AFGHANISTAN AT THE CROSSROADS

Insights on the Conflict

STRATFOR
700 Lavaca Street, Suite 900
Austin, Texas 78701

Printed in the United States of America

The contents of this book originally appeared as analyses
on STRATFOR's subscription Web site.

ISBN: 1452865213
EAN-13: 9781452865218

Publisher: Grant Perry
Editor: Michael McCullar
Project Coordinator: Robert Inks
Designer: TJ Lensing

CONTENTS

CHAPTER 3: THE BORDER

CHAPTER 4: PAKISTAN

CONTENTS

CHAPTER 5: OTHER PLAYERS

ILLUSTRATIONS

TOPOGRAPHY OF AFGHANISTAN

INTRODUCTION

The war in Afghanistan — the American war — has been under way for almost nine years. By its 10th anniversary, on Oct. 7, 2011, Operation Enduring Freedom will have proved to be an enduring operation, the longest major military effort by the United States since the Vietnam War. Launched four weeks after the 9/11 attacks, the Afghanistan campaign removed the Taliban from power and pushed al Qaeda into mountain sanctuaries on the Pakistani side of the border. This did reduce the ability of groups like al Qaeda to operate on Afghan soil, but it did not create a secure and stable Afghanistan that could no longer serve as a launch pad for terrorist attacks against the United States.

Leading up to the U.S. invasion, when the world's sole superpower demanded that the Taliban surrender al Qaeda, the Taliban refused. Although today the two groups are less intertwined, at the time the Taliban — as Islamists — could not surrender another Islamist entity they had grown close to through ideological affinity and loyalty dictated by Pashtun cultural norms. (In any case, in October of 2001, many Afghans did not believe that al Qaeda had perpetrated the 9/11 attacks, and many Muslims do not believe that to this day.)

And despite American perceptions of a quick victory in Afghanistan in the fall of 2001, in reality the Taliban largely declined to fight. There were battles in places like Tora Bora that resulted in significant Taliban losses, but they essentially retreated to their core turf in the south and refused to engage the U.S. war machine on American terms, returning instead to their insurgent roots.

The history of Afghanistan is one of strife, and this history has done much to shape the nation the United States invaded in October 2001. Afghans are more accustomed to perpetual conflict than many cultures — certainly more than the Americans are. The Soviet occupation and war lasted for nearly a decade, throughout the 1980s, and the country quickly descended into an intra-Islamist civil war following the Soviet withdrawal. Even when the Taliban came to power they did not completely rule the country, with the Northern Alliance defying Taliban rule. Nevertheless, the Taliban can be tough and tenacious fighters, and they are working from a well-worn playbook as the United States tries to devise a new solution to a perennial problem.

Indeed, after 9/11 it would have been hard enough for the United States to wage a concerted counterinsurgency against the Taliban even if it had not become so preoccupied with Iraq. After the U.S. invasion of Iraq in March 2003, Afghanistan turned into a backwater theater in the "Global War on Terror." It seemed that the worse things got on the ground in Iraq, the more ground the Taliban regained in Afghanistan. Only after the "Sunni awakening" and U.S. surge in Iraq in 2007 was the United States able to start drawing down its forces in Iraq and refocusing on the Afghan front, where an understrength U.S.-led coalition had been trying to contain the Taliban for years. In 2008, near the end of his presidency, George W. Bush initiated the shift in focus back to Afghanistan, appointing the architect of the Iraqi surge, U.S. Army Gen. David Petraeus, head of U.S. Central Command and putting him in charge of both wars.

A year later, under new U.S. President Barack Obama, U.S. Army Gen. Stanley McChrystal was given his fourth star and command of both U.S. forces and the U.S.-led International Security Assistance Force (ISAF) in Afghanistan. Although a new strategy for Afghanistan would not be publicly announced until near the end of 2009, McChrystal, who previously had been the longest-serving commander of the Joint Special Operations Command, began to make sweeping changes that summer. Then on Dec. 1, 2009, Obama outlined the revamped strategy in a speech at West Point. The plan had three main elements: to maintain pressure on al Qaeda on the

Afghan-Pakistani frontier, to turn back the mounting Taliban offensive by sending 30,000 more American troops to Afghanistan and to train and build up Afghan military forces and civilian structures to assume responsibility after a U.S. withdrawal, which would begin in July 2011.

With Obama's West Point speech and the surge that followed, the war in Afghanistan entered a decisive phase. Gen. McChrystal and the ISAF had an ambitious set of goals — and about 20 months to realize some degree of progress on the ground. The U.S. objective was still to destroy al Qaeda and create a stable and secure Afghanistan, but the strategy was different. Recognizing that the Taliban were an inherent part of the country's political landscape and could not be militarily defeated any time soon, war planners were now distinguishing between reconcilable and irreconcilable elements of the militant movement, in hopes of persuading the former to come to the negotiating table. Meanwhile, the renewed counterinsurgency would focus on key population centers and critical territory while trying to protect and win over the population rather than engaging the Taliban primarily in direct, kinetic operations.

The new U.S. strategy for Afghanistan — perhaps for the first time since 2001 — defined an endgame and exit strategy. Similar to "Vietnamization" under U.S. President Richard Nixon, the Afghanistan plan also emphasized the building up of indigenous security forces and setting them up for success over the next few years, with the explicit intention of handing over responsibility for security to the Afghans. But the goals and the timeline are ambitious and the hurdles are high. The crux of the challenge is time and patience. In his West Point speech, President Obama did not elaborate on the magnitude of the U.S. withdrawal or the date when it would conclude. He made it clear that it would all depend on the situation on the ground. However, he also made it clear that the U.S. commitment to Afghanistan is finite and that there is a limit to how many U.S. lives and dollars will be spent in the legendary graveyard of empires.

The Taliban, on the other hand — patient and persevering — seem to have all the time in the world. And their goals are much more directly obtainable. First they must simply survive, i.e., outlast the United States and its allies. They must also prevent the United States from undermining their support base. To these ends, they will exploit their natural strengths — guerilla warfare, tribal and filial ties with the people and a common interest in a greater role for an ultra-conservative brand of Shariah (Islamic law) in the country's governance. As with any insurgent entity, internal cohesion is an important challenge for the amorphous Taliban, but its leadership considers the movement's position stronger today than it has been since 2001. Mullah Muhammad Omar, the most prominent leader of the Afghan Taliban, is not strictly opposed to a settlement with Kabul, but he firmly believes they can expect some serious concessions in any political reconciliation.

And the ambitious goals the United States has set for itself — the destruction of al Qaeda and the stabilization of Afghanistan — cannot be achieved by coalition forces alone. The U.S. objective in Afghanistan is not the complete destruction of the Taliban's will and ability to resist. In Afghanistan, as in Iraq, the idea is to use military force to reshape the political landscape. And the United States cannot do this without working with other countries outside of the NATO mainstream. In addition to Pakistan, which has long been involved in cultivating a jihadist militancy in the region as a hedge against Indian power, the United States must work with Iran, India, Russia, Turkey, Saudi Arabia, China and Central Asian states, all countries that have interests and/or leverage in Afghanistan. Sooner or later, of course, the Afghan people will have to decide which way they want it to go, and the ISAF has a limited amount of time to provide them the security and space to make that decision.

While a 2011 deadline looms, the military campaign will likely extend beyond that. Any drawdown would begin in mid-2011 and be carefully phased, depending upon the security situation. So there will probably be a sizable American military presence in Afghanistan well into 2012, and perhaps longer. Meanwhile, the United States will be turning its attention to other global matters while the Taliban — a diffuse group of jihadists fighting on their own embattled turf — will be facing some decisions of their own. The Taliban have begun to recognize their strengths just as the Americans have recognized their limitations. It is a critical juncture in the war, and as they prepare to play the long game, the Taliban certainly have time on their side.

STRATFOR
Austin, Texas
May 10, 2010

A NOTE ON CONTENT

STRATFOR presents the following articles as they originally appeared on our subscription Web site, www.STRATFOR.com. These pieces represent some of our best analyses related to the war in Afghanistan since March 2007, organized under chapter headings and presented in the order in which they were published. Since most of the articles were written as individual analyses, there may be overlap from piece to piece and chapter to chapter, and some of the information may seem dated. Naturally, some of the observations herein are linked to a specific time or event that may be years removed from today's situation in Afghanistan. However, STRATFOR believes bringing these pieces together provides valuable insight and perspective on an important geopolitical event.

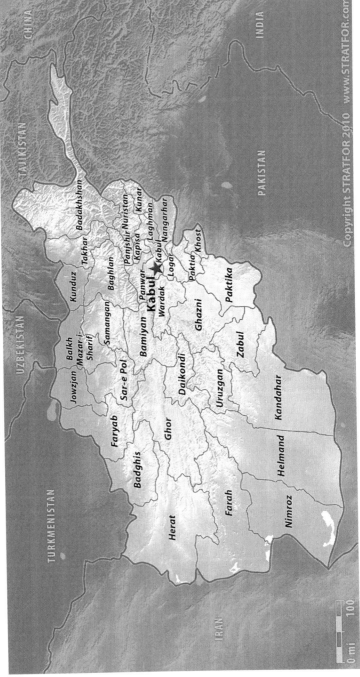

CHAPTER 1: THE UNITED STATES

Fallon and Two Persistent Stalemates
March 12, 2008

In a surprise announcement March 11, U.S. Defense Secretary Robert Gates revealed and accepted the "resignation" of U.S. Central Command (CENTCOM) commander Navy Adm. William J. Fallon. This was no regular personnel shift in Washington, especially since Fallon had held the post for less than a year. With two wars under way and a crisis looming in the Levant, Fallon either resigned in protest or was forced out. The question is why.

The reason is not Iraq, where responsibility and accountability have been shifted squarely to Gen. David Petraeus. Our eyes fall upon the great failure of Fallon's tenure and the far eastern reaches of his area of responsibility: Afghanistan and Pakistan. Fallon's role is largely irrelevant. The underlying issues of Afghanistan and Pakistan predate his tenure. However, the situations in the two countries deteriorated under his supervision.

In Afghanistan, despite its vaunted success, the 2001 U.S. invasion was never really all that successful. The Taliban abandoned Kabul and largely declined to fight, despite some skirmishes and battles between U.S. forces and al Qaeda supporters and other hard-liners. When Washington turned its attention to Iraq, it left a NATO alliance intending to reconstruct the fractured country and a relatively modest military contingent to hunt al Qaeda and Taliban forces.

But the Pentagon never really addressed the complex underlying issues of terrain, ethnicity, tribal loyalty and religious extremism that have left the country ravaged by war for three decades. The only central government Afghanistan has ever known has always relied on tribal loyalty and large military forces. These underlying issues were not clearly evident after U.S. forces kicked in the door in Afghanistan. U.S. forces found calm, since the Taliban declined to fight, and proceeded with reconstruction as Washington's focus shifted to Iraq.

But the Taliban resurged. And in their decentralized, factionalized way they began to make a nuisance of themselves. Then they began adopting tactics that had proved successful in Iraq, like the improvised explosive device. Meanwhile, extremist elements from Pakistan began to pour over the border.

But this was not a one-way vector, and the jihadist insurgency in Afghanistan spilled over into Pakistan, where the insurgency is not only operating from a comparative safe haven but also is compounding political instability in Islamabad and exacerbating the tensions within Pakistani society.

Under Fallon's tenure, in other words, if it did not all come crashing down, it certainly did become apparent to everyone in Washington that the persistent stalemates that had been easy enough to ignore thus far — the military stalemate in Afghanistan and the political stalemate in Pakistan — had become unacceptable and unsustainable.

Fallon's "resignation" was about these same unaddressed problems. STRATFOR's strategic perspective does not often fall to individuals; we see larger forces at work in the world. Fallon did not matter. But the empty seat at CENTCOM is likely to be an exception. Not simply because it is one of the most crucial posts in the U.S. military today, but because of the shift in focus Fallon's removal entails and especially because of the two individuals at the top of the list to replace him: Marine Corps Gen. James Mattis and Petraeus himself.

Petraeus was one of the architects of the "surge" strategy and has overseen its successes thus far. He was also a principal force behind the Army's new counterinsurgency manual. Mattis is something of a legend in the Marines. Not only did he lead Task Force 58 into Afghanistan in 2001, he commanded the 1st Marine Division in Iraq and later the 1st Marine Expeditionary Force during the surge. Petraeus and Mattis worked closely on the new counterinsurgency manual.

These two individuals matter because, since Sept. 11, 2001, they have both solidly established their core competency as counterinsurgency. They do not hesitate to wield military force, but they understand that oftentimes in counterinsurgency the real trick is not bringing that firepower to bear.

The appointment of either man to the top post at CENTCOM has serious implications for the conduct of operations in Afghanistan and the situation in Pakistan. No two contenders for the job are more likely to forgo the current stalemate in Afghanistan and come at the problem with renewed intensity. Indeed, it is the first real telling potential shift in the command of Afghan operations, perhaps since 2001. And neither contender is likely to sit by and let Pakistan continue to simmer, either.

Strategic Divergence: The War Against the Taliban, the War Against Al Qaeda
Jan. 26, 2009

Washington's attention is now zeroing in on Afghanistan. There is talk of doubling U.S. forces there, and preparations are being made for another supply line into Afghanistan — this one running through the former Soviet Union — as an alternative or a supplement to the current Pakistani route. To free up more resources for Afghanistan, the U.S. withdrawal from Iraq probably will be accelerated. And there is discussion about whether the Karzai government serves the purposes of the war in Afghanistan. In short, U.S. President Barack Obama's campaign promise to focus on Afghanistan seems to be taking shape.

We have discussed many aspects of the Afghan war in the past; it is now time to focus on the central issue. What are the strategic goals of the United States in Afghanistan? What resources will be devoted to this mission? What are the intentions and capabilities of the Taliban and others fighting the United States and its NATO allies? Most important, what is the relationship between the war against the Taliban and the war against al Qaeda? If the United States encounters difficulties in the war against the Taliban, will it still be able to contain not only al Qaeda but other terrorist groups? Does the United States need to succeed against the Taliban to be successful against transnational Islamist terrorists? And assuming that U.S. forces are built up in Afghanistan and that the supply problem through Pakistan is solved, are the defeat of Taliban and the disruption of al Qaeda likely?

Al Qaeda and U.S. Goals Post-9/11

The overarching goal of the United States since Sept. 11, 2001, has been to prevent further attacks by al Qaeda in the United States. Washington has used two means toward this end. One was defensive, aimed at increasing the difficulty of al Qaeda operatives to penetrate and operate within the United States. The second was to attack and destroy al Qaeda prime, the group around Osama bin Laden that organized and executed 9/11 and other attacks in Europe. It is this group — not other groups that call themselves al Qaeda but only are able to operate in the countries where they were formed — that was the target of the United States, because this was the group that had demonstrated the ability to launch intercontinental strikes.

Al Qaeda prime had its main headquarters in Afghanistan. It was not an Afghan group, but one drawn from multiple Islamic countries. It was in alliance with an Afghan group, the Taliban. The Taliban had won a civil war in Afghanistan, creating a coalition of support among tribes that had given the group control, direct or indirect, over most of the country. It is important to remember that al Qaeda was separate from the Taliban; the former was a multinational force, while the Taliban were an internal Afghan political power.

The United States has two strategic goals in Afghanistan. The first is to destroy the remnants of al Qaeda prime — the central command of al Qaeda — in Afghanistan. The second is to use Afghanistan as a base for destroying al Qaeda in Pakistan and to prevent the return of al Qaeda to Afghanistan.

To achieve these goals, Washington has sought to make Afghanistan inhospitable to al Qaeda. The United States forced the Taliban from Afghanistan's main cities and into the countryside, and established a new, anti-Taliban government in Kabul under President Hamid Karzai. Washington intended to deny al Qaeda bases in Afghanistan by unseating the Taliban government, creating a new pro-American government and then using Afghanistan as a base against al Qaeda in Pakistan.

The United States succeeded in forcing the Taliban from power in the sense that in giving up the cities, the Taliban lost formal control of the country. To be more precise, early in the U.S. attack in 2001, the Taliban realized that the massed defense of Afghan cities was impossible in the face of American air power. The ability of U.S. B-52s to devastate any concentration of forces meant that the Taliban could not defend the cities, but had to withdraw, disperse and reform its units for combat on more favorable terms.

At this point, we must separate the fates of al Qaeda and the Taliban. During the Taliban retreat, al Qaeda had to retreat as well. Since the United States lacked sufficient force to destroy al Qaeda at Tora Bora, al Qaeda was able to retreat into northwestern Pakistan. There, it enjoys the advantages of terrain, superior tactical intelligence and support networks.

Even so, in nearly eight years of war, U.S. intelligence and special operations forces have maintained pressure on al Qaeda in Pakistan. The United States has imposed attrition on al Qaeda, disrupting its command, control and communications and isolating it. In the process, the United States used one of al Qaeda's operational principles against it. To avoid penetration by hostile intelligence services, al Qaeda has not recruited new cadres for its primary unit. This makes it very difficult to develop intelligence on al Qaeda, but it also makes it impossible for al Qaeda to replace its losses. Thus, in a long war of attrition, every loss imposed on al Qaeda has been irreplaceable, and over time, al Qaeda prime declined dramatically in effectiveness — meaning it has been years since it has carried out an effective operation.

The situation was very different with the Taliban. The Taliban, it is essential to recall, won the Afghan civil war that followed the Soviet withdrawal despite Russian and Iranian support for its opponents. That means the Taliban have a great deal of support and a strong infrastructure, and, above all, they are resilient. After the group withdrew from Afghanistan's cities and lost formal power post-9/11, it still retained a great deal of informal influence — if not control — over large regions of Afghanistan and in areas across the border in Pakistan. Over the years since the U.S. invasion, the Taliban have regrouped, rearmed and increased their operations in Afghanistan. And the conflict with the Taliban has now become a conventional guerrilla war.

The Taliban and Guerrilla Warfare

The Taliban have forged relationships among many Afghan (and Pakistani) tribes. These tribes have been alienated by Karzai and the Americans, and far more important, they do not perceive the Americans and Karzai as potential winners in the Afghan conflict. They recall the Russian and British defeats. The tribes have long memories, and they know that foreigners don't stay very long. Betting on the United States and Karzai — when the United States has sent only 30,000 troops to Afghanistan, and is struggling with the idea of sending another 30,000 troops — does not strike them as prudent. The United States is behaving like a power not planning to win; and, in any event, the tribes would not be much impressed if the Americans *were* planning to win.

The tribes therefore do not want to get on the wrong side of the Taliban. That means they aid and shelter Taliban forces, and provide them intelligence on enemy movement and intentions. With their base camps and supply lines running from Pakistan, the Taliban are thus in a position to recruit, train and arm an increasingly large force.

The Taliban have the classic advantage of guerrillas operating in known terrain with a network of supporters: superior intelligence. They know where the Americans are, what the Americans are doing and when the Americans are going to strike. The Taliban decline combat on unfavorable terms and strike when and where the Americans are weakest. The Americans, on the other hand, have the classic problem of counterinsurgency: They enjoy superior force and firepower, and can defeat anyone they can locate and pin down, but they lack intelligence. As much as technical intelligence from unmanned aerial vehicles and satellites is useful, human intelligence is the only effective long-term solution to defeating an insurgency. In this, the Taliban have the advantage: They have been there longer, they are in more places and they are not going anywhere.

There is no conceivable force the United States can deploy to pacify Afghanistan. A possible alternative is moving into Pakistan to cut the supply lines and destroy the Taliban's base camps. The problem is that if the Americans lack the troops to successfully operate in Afghanistan, it is even less likely they have the troops to operate in both Afghanistan and Pakistan. The United States could use the Korean War example, taking responsibility for cutting the Taliban off from supplies and reinforcements from Pakistan, but that assumes that the Afghan government has an effective force motivated to engage and defeat the Taliban. The Afghan government doesn't.

The obvious American solution — or at least the best available solution — is to retreat to strategic Afghan points and cities and protect the Karzai regime. The problem here is that in Afghanistan, holding the cities doesn't provide the key to the country; rather, holding the countryside provides the key to the cities. Moreover, a purely defensive posture opens the United States up to the Dien Bien Phu/

Khe Sanh counterstrategy, in which guerrillas shift to positional warfare, isolate a base and try to overrun it.

A purely defensive posture could create a stalemate, but nothing more. That stalemate could create the foundations for political negotiations, but if there is no threat to the enemy, the enemy has little reason to negotiate. Therefore, there must be strikes against Taliban concentrations. The problem is that the Taliban know that concentration is suicide, and so they work to deny the Americans valuable targets. The United States can exhaust itself attacking minor targets based on poor intelligence. It won't get anywhere.

U.S. Strategy and al Qaeda's Diminution

From the beginning, the Karzai government has failed to take control of the countryside. Therefore, al Qaeda has had the option to redeploy into Afghanistan if it chose. It didn't because it is risk-averse. That may seem like a strange thing to say about a group that flies planes into buildings, but what it means is that the group's members are relatively few, so al Qaeda cannot risk operational failures. It thus keeps its powder dry and stays in hiding.

This then frames the U.S. strategic question. The United States has no intrinsic interest in the nature of the Afghan government. The United States is interested in making certain the Taliban do not provide sanctuary to al Qaeda prime. But it is not clear that al Qaeda prime is operational anymore. Some members remain, putting out videos now and then and trying to appear fearsome, but it would seem that U.S. operations have crippled al Qaeda.

So if the primary reason for fighting the Taliban is to keep al Qaeda prime from having a base of operations in Afghanistan, that reason might be moot now since al Qaeda appears to be wrecked. This is not to say that another Islamist terrorist group could not arise and develop the sophisticated methods and training of al Qaeda prime. But such a group could deploy many places, and in any case, obtaining the needed skills in moving money, holding covert meetings and the like is much harder than it looks — and with many intelligence services, including those in the Islamic world, on the lookout for this, recruitment would be hard.

It is therefore no longer clear that resisting the Taliban is essential for blocking al Qaeda: Al Qaeda may simply no longer be there. (At this point, the burden of proof is on those who think al Qaeda remains operational.)

Two things emerge from this. First, the search for al Qaeda and other Islamist groups is an intelligence matter best left to the covert capabilities of U.S. intelligence and Special Operations Command. Defeating al Qaeda does not require tens of thousands of troops — it requires excellent intelligence and a special operations capability. That is true whether al Qaeda is in Pakistan or Afghanistan. Intelligence, covert forces and airstrikes are what is needed in this fight, and of the three, intelligence is the key.

Second, the current strategy in Afghanistan cannot secure Afghanistan, nor does it materially contribute to shutting down al Qaeda. Trying to hold some cities and strategic points with the number of troops currently under consideration is not an effective strategy to this end; the United States is already ceding large areas of Afghanistan to the Taliban that could serve as sanctuary for al Qaeda. Protecting the Karzai government and key cities is therefore not significantly contributing to the al Qaeda-suppression strategy.

In sum, the United States does not control enough of Afghanistan to deny al Qaeda sanctuary, it cannot control the border with Pakistan and it lacks effective intelligence and troops for defeating the Taliban.

Logic argues, therefore, for the creation of a political process for the withdrawal of U.S. forces from Afghanistan coupled with a recommitment to intelligence operations against al Qaeda. Ultimately, the United States must protect itself from radical Islamists, but it cannot create a united, pro-American Afghanistan. That would not happen even if the United States sent 500,000 troops there, which it doesn't have anyway.

A Tale of Two Surges

The U.S. strategy now appears to involve trying a surge, or sending in more troops and negotiating with the Taliban, mirroring the strategy used in Iraq. But the problem with that strategy is that the Taliban don't seem inclined to make concessions to the United States. The Taliban don't think the United States can win, and they know the United States won't stay. The Petraeus strategy is to inflict enough pain on the Taliban to cause them to rethink their position, which worked in Iraq. But it did not work in Vietnam. So long as the Taliban have resources flowing and can survive American attacks, they will calculate that they can outlast the Americans. This has been Afghan strategy for centuries, and it worked against the British and Russians.

If it works against the Americans, too, splitting the al Qaeda strategy from the Taliban strategy will be the inevitable outcome for the United States. In that case, the CIA will become the critical war fighter in the theater, while conventional forces will be withdrawn. It follows that Obama will need to think carefully about his approach to intelligence.

This is not an argument that al Qaeda is no longer a threat, although the threat appears diminished. Nor is it an argument that dealing with terrorism in Afghanistan and Pakistan is not a priority. Instead, it is an argument that the defeat of the Taliban under rationally anticipated circumstances is unlikely and that a negotiated settlement in Afghanistan will be much more difficult and unlikely than the settlement was in Iraq — but that even so, a robust effort against Islamist terror groups must continue regardless of the outcome of the war with the Taliban.

Therefore, we expect that the United States will separate the two conflicts in response to these realities. This will mean that containing terrorists will not be dependent on defeating or holding out against the Taliban, holding Afghanistan's cities, or preserving the Karzai regime. We expect the United States to surge troops into Afghanistan, but in due course, the counterterrorist portion will diverge from the counter-Taliban portion. The counterterrorist portion will be maintained as an intense covert operation, while the overt operation will wind down over time. The Taliban ruling Afghanistan is not a threat to the United States, so long as intense counterterrorist operations continue there.

The cost of failure in Afghanistan is simply too high and the connection to counterterrorist activities too tenuous for the two strategies to be linked. And since the counterterror war is already distinct from conventional operations in much of Afghanistan and Pakistan, our forecast is not really that radical.

Hurry Up and Wait
Feb. 17, 2009

Reports emerged Feb. 17 that U.S. President Barack Obama will soon make an announcement authorizing the deployment of 17,000 additional troops to Afghanistan. There are roughly 60,000 U.S. and NATO troops there now (split about evenly). Nearly 3,000 soldiers of the 3rd Brigade Combat Team (BCT) of the U.S. Army's 10th Mountain Division — the first additional unit to arrive as part of the surge strategy — landed in January. An additional 17,000 troops (first 8,000 Marines, followed by 9,000 soldiers) would bring the total to about 50,000 U.S. troops in Afghanistan. Taking into account NATO forces, this would still be almost 30,000 shy of the peak Soviet military presence that failed to subdue U.S.-backed Islamist rebels in the country in the 1980s.

The 3rd BCT is already engaged in combat outside Kabul, and this fighting will only escalate as the weather improves. Beginning in March, the spring thaw in Afghanistan traditionally marks the beginning of campaign season as insurgents become more mobile. Attacks in Kabul and on supply routes in Pakistan already have increased, and Washington is trying to lock down alternative supply routes (part of broader negotiations with Russia) as U.S. and NATO forces face an entrenched insurgency that has extensive tribal contacts, support and refuge on the Pakistani side of the border.

Any surge in U.S./NATO troops and any increase in operational tempo will require a significant expansion of supporting infrastructure and supplies. As a proportion of forces already in country, the most aggressive proposed surge into Afghanistan would be much larger than the surge into Iraq. This means that existing infrastructure and supply lines will be even more heavily taxed than the ones in Iraq, even as these supply lines grow increasingly vulnerable and negotiations on alternatives continue to drag on. (Indeed, last week Bishkek threatened to close the heavily utilized air base at Manas in Kyrgyzstan.) The surge into Afghanistan has been anticipated, preparations are under way and the Pakistani supply lines remain open — if increasingly tenuous. But March is fast approaching.

The Iraq surge provides an increasingly stark contrast to the proposed surge in Afghanistan (which, granted, will not simply be a cut-and-paste repeat of the Iraq strategy). Although the surge in Iraq was controversial, then-President George W. Bush was able to work from an already-defined strategy to move in decisive reinforcements over the course of five months. By this time in 2007, the second of five BCTs had already arrived in country. Commanders had a clear sense of the mission, the additional forces they would receive and the timetable on which they would arrive. Supply lines were short and secure.

But in Afghanistan, seasonal changes are far more extreme than those in Iraq, and they are compounded by high altitudes and rugged terrain. Hence, operational timing in Afghanistan is much more critical. Ideally, had there not been a U.S. presidential transition over the last few months, and had the Army deployment rotation schedule not been still reeling from the Iraq surge, a surge to Afghanistan would already be in place, with fresh forces taking advantage of the winter lull to establish security around the capital and, as spring took hold, to begin securing surrounding territory. Positioning forces before campaign season would maximize the time available to succeed before the next Afghan winter rolled around.

The reality is that the strategy and force structure of a surge in Afghanistan have continued to be formulated even after the surge began, and deployment of the additional 17,000 troops reportedly will not be complete until late summer (in time for Afghan elections in August).

In Iraq, history may well decide that the stars finally aligned for an effective surge of U.S. military force, which could be credited with breaking the cycle of violence long enough to allow for political accommodation. It is not at all clear how the stars will align in the Afghan theater, which is beset by cross-border issues with Pakistan, and where governments in Kabul and Islamabad are wracked with infighting and myriad other internal problems. Indeed, the deteriorating conditions in both countries are inextricably linked, and any security gains and tactical victories made thanks to more U.S. boots on the ground in Afghanistan might make little difference.

The Difficulties of Talking to the Taliban
March 11, 2009

Afghanistan's Taliban on March 10 rejected U.S. President Barack Obama's idea of reaching out to moderates within the movement, calling it "illogical." When asked whether Taliban chief Mullah Mohammad Omar had a response to Obama's proposal, spokesman Qari Mohammad Yousuf said, "This does not require any response or reaction, for this is illogical." Yousuf said he did not know what Obama meant by the term "moderate Taliban," adding, "If it means those who are not fighting and are sitting in their homes, then talking to them is meaningless. This really is surprising the Taliban."

The comments came in response to statements Obama made in a New York Times interview, published March 8. He said Washington was not winning the war in Afghanistan, which makes it necessary to open a dialogue with the insurgents, as was done in Iraq.

The Taliban reaction is expected and fits with their efforts to shape global perceptions in a way that serves their objectives. The comment about what constitutes "moderate Taliban," however, has caught our attention. It raises questions about what engaging the Taliban would entail, and about the huge contrast between the environment in Afghanistan and Gen. David Petraeus' experience in Iraq, where his efforts to engage the Sunnis defused the insurgency there. Obama's plan would hardly be the first attempt to reach out to "moderate Taliban" — a process Washington engaged in as early as five years ago, with few results.

A comparison of the insurgencies in Iraq and Afghanistan is a useful starting point for understanding what talks with the Taliban would look like.

In Iraq, the jihadists were foreigners who depended on their Sunni hosts, whereas in Afghanistan, the Pashtun jihadists are bona fide Afghan nationals. Furthermore, Iraq's Sunni tribal leadership wielded great influence over nationalist Iraqis who joined the insurgency — and this allowed the Sunnis to launch a successful campaign against al Qaeda after striking a deal with Washington. In Afghanistan, however, the Taliban are more powerful than the tribal chiefs. Sectarian differences within Iraq made it possible for the United States to bring the Sunni insurgency to a halt. Because the Sunnis feared the Shia and their Iranian patrons, they opted to align with the United States. But the sectarian dynamic is practically nonexistent in Afghanistan.

These stark differences in the two insurgent landscapes raise the question of how one goes about talking to the Taliban. It should be borne in mind that "Taliban" is no longer the name of a single organization, but rather describes a phenomenon that includes a wide range of Pashtun Islamist militants who operate in neighboring Pakistan as well as Afghanistan. In other words, there is no single point of contact with whom meaningful negotiations could be conducted — assuming that some within the Taliban are interested in talks.

The simple act of making contact with the other side requires intermediaries who carry some level of influence with the insurgents. In the case of the Taliban, the powers with the closest ties are

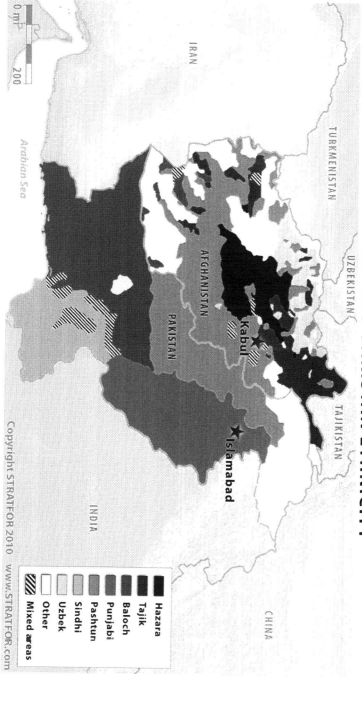

AFGHANISTAN AND PAKISTAN ETHNICITY

Hazara
Tajik
Baloch
Punjabi
Pashtun
Sindhi
Uzbek
Other
Mixed areas

0 mi 200

Copyright STRATFOR 2010   www.STRATFOR.com

Pakistan and Saudi Arabia — the two key states that recognized the Taliban government that ruled Afghanistan between 1996 and 2001.

The Pakistan option is problematic for several reasons. First, Islamabad's influence over the Taliban is no longer what it used to be, given the Talibanization of its own territory. Second, Pakistan shares influence over the Taliban with al Qaeda. This means that Islamabad's Taliban allies have ties to al Qaeda, which defeats the purpose of negotiations: trying to split the Taliban from al Qaeda and the transnational jihadists. Third, there is huge mistrust in Washington regarding Islamabad's intent and capabilities, which has led the United States to carry out growing numbers of unilateral strikes against jihadists on Pakistani territory.

That leaves Saudi Arabia as the only potential intermediary. But there is still no avoiding the Pakistanis, because the Saudis also rely upon them for access to the Taliban movement. And even if these hurdles can be overcome and a process to politically engage the Taliban can be started, with Saudi and Pakistani involvement, other difficulties would remain. Specifically, there would be problems with Iran, which has significant influence in Afghanistan and to whom the United States is already reaching out as a potential ally on Afghanistan. Tehran views the Taliban as an enemy, but the regime also is angered by the U.S.-Saudi alignment against it in the Middle East. Consequently, the United States will have to balance between Iran and Sunni powers regarding Afghanistan — much as it is doing regarding Iraq.

In essence, any future Afghan settlement designed to prevent the place from being a sanctuary for transnational jihadists will entail a complex international arrangement involving both state and non-state actors. Clearly, there is a huge prerequisite: The United States must get all concerned parties on board with the plan. For now, though, Washington is still learning about the various parts of the process.

Obama's Plan and the Key Battleground
Dec. 2, 2009

U.S. President Barack Obama announced the broad structure of his Afghanistan strategy in a speech at West Point on Dec. 1. The strategy had three core elements. First, he intends to maintain pressure on al Qaeda on the Afghan-Pakistani border and in other regions of the world. Second, he intends to blunt the Taliban offensive by sending an additional 30,000 American troops to Afghanistan, in hopes that an unspecified number of NATO troops will join them. Third, he will use the space created by the counteroffensive against the Taliban and the resulting security in some regions of Afghanistan to train and build Afghan military forces and civilian structures to assume responsibility after the United States withdraws. Obama added that the U.S. withdrawal will begin in July 2011, but provided neither information on the magnitude of the withdrawal nor the date when the withdrawal would conclude. He made it clear that these will depend on the situation on the ground, adding that the U.S. commitment is finite.

In understanding this strategy, we must begin with an obvious but unstated point: The extra forces that will be deployed to Afghanistan are not expected to defeat the Taliban. Instead, their mission is to reverse the momentum of previous years and to create the circumstances under which an Afghan force can take over the mission. The U.S. presence is therefore a stopgap measure, not the ultimate solution.

The ultimate solution is training an Afghan force to engage the Taliban over the long haul, undermining support for the Taliban, and dealing with al Qaeda forces along the Pakistani border and in the rest of Afghanistan. If the United States withdraws all of its forces as Obama intends, the Afghan military would have to assume all of these missions. Therefore, we must consider the condition of the Afghan military to evaluate the strategy's viability.

Afghanistan and Vietnam

Obama went to great pains to distinguish Afghanistan from Vietnam, and there are indeed many differences. The core strategy adopted by Richard Nixon (not Lyndon Johnson) in Vietnam, called "Vietnamization," saw U.S. forces working to blunt and disrupt the main North Vietnamese forces while the Army of the Republic of Vietnam (ARVN) would be trained, motivated and deployed to replace U.S. forces, which would be systematically withdrawn from Vietnam. The equivalent of the Afghan surge was the U.S. attack on North Vietnamese Army (NVA) bases in Cambodia and offensives in northern South Vietnam designed to disrupt NVA command and control and logistics and forestall a major offensive by the NVA. Troops were in fact removed in parallel with these offensives.

Nixon faced two points Obama now faces. First, the United States could not provide security for South Vietnam indefinitely. Second, the South Vietnamese would have to provide security for themselves. The role of the United States was to create the conditions under which the ARVN would become an effective fighting force; the impending U.S. withdrawal was intended to increase the pressure on the Vietnamese government to reform and on the ARVN to fight.

Many have argued that the core weakness of the strategy was that the ARVN was not motivated to fight. This was certainly true in some cases, but the idea that the South Vietnamese were generally sympathetic to the Communists is untrue. Some were, but many weren't, as shown by the minimal refugee movement into NVA-held territory or into North Vietnam itself contrasted with the substantial refugee movement into U.S./ARVN-held territory and away from NVA forces. The patterns of refugee movement are, we think, highly indicative of true sentiment.

Certainly, there were mixed sentiments, but the failure of the ARVN was not primarily due to hostility or even lack of motivation. Instead, it was due to a problem that must be addressed and overcome if the war in Afghanistan is to succeed. That problem is understanding the role that Communist sympathizers and agents played in the formation of the ARVN.

By the time the ARVN expanded — and for that matter from its very foundation — the North Vietnamese intelligence services had created a systematic program for inserting operatives and recruiting sympathizers at every level of the ARVN, from senior staff and command positions down to the squad level. The exploitation of these assets was not random nor merely intended to undermine morale. Instead, it provided the NVA with strategic, operational and tactical intelligence on ARVN operations, and when ARVN and U.S. forces operated together, on U.S. efforts as well.

In any insurgency, the key for insurgent victory is avoiding battles on the enemy's terms and initiating combat only on the insurgents' terms. The NVA was a light infantry force. The ARVN — and the U.S. Army on which it was modeled — was a much heavier, combined-arms force. In any encounter between the NVA and its enemies the NVA would lose unless the encounter was at the time and place of the NVA's choosing. ARVN and U.S. forces had a tremendous advantage in firepower and sheer weight. But they had a significant weakness: The weight they bought to bear meant they were less agile. The NVA had a tremendous weakness. Caught by surprise, it would be defeated. And it had a great advantage: Its intelligence network inside the ARVN generally kept it from being surprised. It also revealed weakness in its enemies' deployment, allowing it to initiate successful offensives.

All war is about intelligence, but nowhere is this truer than in counterinsurgency and guerrilla war, where invisibility to the enemy and maintaining the initiative in all engagements is key. Only clear intelligence on the enemy's capability gives this initiative to an insurgent, and only denying intelligence to the enemy — or knowing what the enemy knows and intends — preserves the insurgent force.

The construction of an Afghan military is an obvious opportunity for Taliban operatives and sympathizers to be inserted into the force. As in Vietnam, such operatives and sympathizers are not readily distinguishable from loyal soldiers; ideology is not something easy to discern. With these operatives in place, the Taliban will know of and avoid Afghan army forces and will identify Afghan army weaknesses. Knowing that the Americans are withdrawing, as the NVA knew in Vietnam, means the rational strategy of the Taliban is to reduce operational tempo, allow the withdrawal to proceed, and then take advantage of superior intelligence and the ability to disrupt the Afghan forces internally to launch the Taliban offensives.

The Western solution is not to prevent Taliban sympathizers from penetrating the Afghan army. Rather, the solution is penetrating the Taliban. In Vietnam, the United States used signals intelligence extensively. The NVA came to understand this and minimized radio communications, accepting inefficient central command and control in return for operational security. The solution to this problem lay in placing South Vietnamese into the NVA. There were many cases in which this worked, but on balance, the NVA had a huge advantage in the length of time it had spent penetrating the ARVN versus U.S. and ARVN counteractions. The intelligence war on the whole went to the North Vietnamese. The United States won almost all engagements, but the NVA made certain that it avoided most engagements until it was ready.

In the case of Afghanistan, the United States has far more sophisticated intelligence-gathering tools than it did in Vietnam. Nevertheless, the basic principle remains: An intelligence tool can be understood, taken into account and evaded. By contrast, deep penetration on multiple levels by human intelligence cannot be avoided.

Pakistan's Role

Obama mentioned Pakistan's critical role. Clearly, he understands the lessons of Vietnam regarding sanctuary, and so he made it clear that he expects Pakistan to engage and destroy Taliban forces on its territory and to deny Afghan Taliban supplies, replacements and refuge. He cited the Swat and South Waziristan offensives as examples of the Pakistanis' growing effectiveness. While this is a significant piece of his strategy, the Pakistanis must play another role with regard to intelligence.

The heart of Obama's strategy lies not in the surge, but rather in turning the war over to the Afghans. As in Vietnam, any simplistic model of loyalties doesn't work. There are Afghans sufficiently motivated to form the core of an effective army. As in Vietnam, the problem is that this army will contain large numbers of Taliban sympathizers; there is no way to prevent this. The Taliban are not stupid. They have moved and will continue to move their people into as many key positions as possible.

The challenge lies in leveling the playing field by inserting operatives into the Taliban. Since the Afghan intelligence services are inherently insecure, they can't carry out such missions. American personnel bring technical intelligence to bear, but that does not compensate for human intelligence. The only entity that could conceivably penetrate the Taliban and remain secure is the Pakistani Inter-Services Intelligence (ISI). This would give the Americans and Afghans knowledge of Taliban plans and deployments. This would diminish the ability of the Taliban to evade attacks, and although penetrated as well, the Afghan army would enjoy a chance the ARVN never had.

But only the ISI could do this, and thinking of the ISI as secure is hard to do from a historical point of view. The ISI worked closely with the Taliban during the Afghan civil war that brought it to power and afterwards, and the ISI had many Taliban sympathizers. The ISI underwent significant purging and restructuring to eliminate these elements in recent years, but no one knows how successful these efforts were.

The ISI remains the center of the entire problem. If the war is about creating an Afghan army, and if we accept that the Taliban will penetrate this army heavily no matter what, then the only counter is to penetrate the Taliban equally. Without that, Obama's entire strategy fails as Nixon's did.

In his talk, Obama quite properly avoided discussing the intelligence aspect of the war. He clearly cannot ignore the problem we have laid out, but neither can he simply count on the ISI. He does not need the entire ISI for this mission, however. He needs a carved out portion — compartmentalized and invisible to the greatest possible extent — to recruit and insert operatives into the Taliban and to create and manage communication networks so as to render the Taliban transparent. Given Taliban successes of late, it isn't clear whether he has this intelligence capability. Either way, we would have to assume that some Pakistani solution to the Taliban intelligence issue has been discussed (and such a solution must be Pakistani for ethnic and linguistic reasons).

Every war has its center of gravity, and Obama has made clear that the center of gravity of this war will be the Afghan military's ability to replace the Americans in a very few years. If that is the center of gravity, and if maintaining security against Taliban penetration is impossible, then the single most important enabler to Obama's strategy would seem to be the ability to make the Taliban transparent.

Therefore, Pakistan is important not only as the Cambodia of this war, the place where insurgents go to regroup and resupply, but also as a key element of the solution to the intelligence war. It is all about Pakistan. And that makes Obama's plan difficult to execute. It is far easier to write these words than to execute a plan based on them. But to the extent Obama is serious about the Afghan army taking over, he and his team have had to think about how to do this.

The Evolution of a Strategy
Dec. 2, 2009

U.S. President Barack Obama articulated his strategy for Afghanistan on Dec. 1 in a much-anticipated speech at the U.S. Military Academy at West Point. In it, he provided an endgame and an exit strategy for the U.S. and NATO mission there, and this is no small development. Following the 9/11 attacks, the United States scrambled to move forces into Afghanistan as quickly as possible, since it had little understanding of al Qaeda's true capabilities. By necessity, little thought was given to a long-term strategy for the country — even as the Taliban largely declined to fight and withdrew into the rugged countryside. Despite some significant and hard-fought battles, they were hardly "defeated."

At the same time, even as the battle of Tora Bora was being fought in the mountains of eastern Afghanistan in December 2001, the White House was eyeing Iraq. By 2002, Baghdad had become the primary focus of the U.S. military, which was marshalling its resources and setting the stage for an invasion that would ultimately take place in March 2003. Meanwhile, the United States continued to conduct counterterrorism operations in Afghanistan — its primary strategic objective in the country. While security operations and reconstruction efforts were certainly being conducted, the number of U.S. troops in Afghanistan began to creep above 10,000 only as 2003 ended.

As Iraq began to sour in the years that followed, Washington became increasingly preoccupied with the mission there. This is not to say that the Afghan campaign was devoid of strategic direction, but with so much at stake in Iraq, the reality was that Afghanistan was a secondary priority and efforts there were necessarily constrained by forces and focus committed elsewhere. Iraq began to absorb more and more U.S. military resources as the Taliban began to resurge in Afghanistan. While U.K. and Canadian forces began engaging in heavy fighting against the Taliban in 2006 in the country's southwestern provinces of Kandahar and Helmand, the United States was committing additional forces (even before the surge that began in early 2007) to the fight in Iraq.

Even while this surge was taking place, it was becoming clear that the Taliban resurgence was reaching an unacceptable level. In March 2008, as U.S. forces were beginning to draw down in Iraq, U.S. Central Command commander Navy Adm. William J. Fallon was forced out of the job and replaced by Gen. David Petraeus, the commander in Iraq who oversaw the surge there. It was a clear move to shift the focus back to Afghanistan.

But while Petraeus was quick to advocate a counterinsurgency focus, he was forced to admit early on that the political reconciliation that allowed the surge to succeed in Iraq would be more problematic in Afghanistan. The United States did not have the nuanced and sophisticated understanding of the Taliban to even identify — much less compel — reconcilable elements of the Taliban who might be amenable to political accommodation to sit down at the table. At the same time, as Obama emphasized in his speech, a counterinsurgency strategy would take a decade or more and a larger commitment of U.S. troops and support than anyone is suggesting be committed to the country.

In May 2009, early in Obama's presidency, Gen. Stanley McChrystal was nominated for command in Afghanistan and quickly began to make changes to the tactics and rules of engagement consistent with the counterinsurgency focus. Though McChrystal began his tenure emphasizing to commanders that they had an extremely limited window in which to demonstrate results, these shifts were largely tactical and operational rather than strategic in nature.

McChrystal was put in place to shake things up, and it was only later that a strategic review at the White House really began. But as the White House continued to come to grips with the intractable challenges of Afghanistan and the deteriorating military and political situation there (and in Pakistan), McChrystal continued to push forward with changes to the way U.S. and NATO forces were doing business in Afghanistan even as he was helping to define the ultimate strategic objectives.

While defending the population and training indigenous security forces were already key focal points of McChrystal's efforts, what Obama's new plan does — perhaps for the first time since 2001 — is define an endgame and an exit strategy. Similar to Vietnamization under U.S. President Richard Nixon, Obama's plan makes the building up of indigenous security forces and setting them up for success the primary focus of the next few years, with the explicit intention of handing over responsibility for security to the Afghans. While this was certainly part of McChrystal's ultimate plan, it was only on Dec.

1 that the mission was clearly defined and a broad timetable described (though it contains considerable wiggle room, and a re-evaluation in December 2010 will further refine the plan).

There is no further ambiguity. The U.S. military and its NATO allies have their marching orders. The issues now are achievability and execution, not strategy selection.

The New U.S. Strategy in Afghanistan
Feb. 15, 2010

In the aftermath of the 9/11 attacks, the United States entered Afghanistan to conduct a limited war with a limited objective: defeat al Qaeda and prevent Afghanistan from ever again serving as a sanctuary for any transnational terrorist group bent on attacking the United States. STRATFOR has long held that the former goal has been achieved, in effect, and what remains of al Qaeda prime — the group's core leadership — is not in Afghanistan but across the border in Pakistan. While pressure must be kept on that leadership to prevent the group from regaining its former operational capability, this is an objective very different from the one the United States and International Security Assistance Force (ISAF) are currently pursuing.

The current U.S. strategy in Afghanistan is to use military force, as the United States did in Iraq, to reshape the political landscape. Everyone from President Barack Obama to Gen. Stanley McChrystal has made it clear that the United States has no interest in making the investment of American resources necessary to carry out a decade-long (or longer) counterinsurgency and nation-building campaign. Instead, the United States has found itself in a place in which it has found itself many times before: involved in a conflict for which its original intention for entering no longer holds and without a clear strategy for extricating itself from that conflict.

This is not about "winning" or "losing." The primary strategic goal of the United States in Afghanistan has little to do with the hearts and minds of the Afghan people. That may be an important means but it is not a strategic end. With a resurgent Russia, a perpetually defiant Iran and an ongoing global financial crisis — not to mention profound pressures at home — the grand strategic objective of the United States in Afghanistan must ultimately be withdrawal. This does not mean total withdrawal. Advisers and counterterrorism forces are indeed likely to remain in Afghanistan for some time. But the European commitment to the war is waning fast, and the United States has felt the strain of having its ground combat forces almost completely absorbed far too long.

To facilitate that withdrawal, the United States is trying to establish sustainable conditions — to the extent possible — that are conducive to longer-term U.S. interests in the region. Still paramount among these interests is sanctuary denial, and the United States has no intention of leaving Afghanistan only to watch it again become a haven for transnational terrorists. Hence, it is working now to shape conditions on the ground before leaving.

Immediate and total withdrawal would surrender the country to the Taliban at a time when the Taliban's power is already on the rise. Not only would this give the movement that was driven from power in Kabul in 2001 an opportunity to wage a civil war and attempt to regain power (the Taliban realize that returning to their status of the 1990s is unlikely), it would also leave a government in Kabul with little real control over much of the country, relieving the pressure on al Qaeda in the Afghan-Pakistani border region and emboldening parallel insurgencies in Pakistan.

The United States is patently unwilling to commit the forces necessary to impose a military reality on Afghanistan (likely half a million troops or more, though no one really knows how many it would take, since it has never been done). Instead, military force is being applied in order to break cycles of violence, rebalance the security dynamic in key areas, shift perceptions and carve out space in which a political accommodation can take place.

In terms of military strategy, this means clearing, holding and building (though there is precious little time for building) in key population centers and Taliban strongholds like Helmand province. The idea is to secure the population from Taliban intimidation while denying the Taliban key bases of popular support (from which it draws not only safe haven but also recruits and financial resources). The ultimate goal is to create reasonably secure conditions under which popular support of provincial and district governments can be encouraged without the threat of reprisal and from which effective local security forces can deploy to establish long-term control.

The key aspect of this strategy is "Vietnamization" — working in conjunction with and expanding Afghan National Army (ANA) and Afghan National Police (ANP) forces to establish security and increasingly take the lead in day-to-day security operations. (The term was coined in the early 1970s, when U.S. President Richard Nixon drew down the American involvement in Vietnam by transitioning the ground combat role to Vietnamese forces.) In any counterinsurgency, effective indigenous forces are more valuable, in many ways, than foreign troops, which are less sensitive to cultural norms and local nuances and are seen by the population as outsiders.

But the real objective of the military strategy in Afghanistan is political. Gen. McChrystal has even said explicitly that he believes "that a political solution to all conflicts is the inevitable outcome." Though the objective of the use of military force almost always comes down to political goals, the kind of campaign being conducted in Afghanistan is particularly challenging. The goal is not the complete destruction of the enemy's will and ability to resist (as it was, for example, in World War II). In Afghanistan, as in Iraq, the objective is far more subtle than that: it is to use military force to reshape the political landscape. The key challenge in Afghanistan is that the insurgents — the Taliban — are not a small group of discrete individuals like the remnants of al Qaeda prime. The movement is diffuse and varied, itself part of the political landscape that must be reshaped, and the entire movement cannot be removed from the equation.

At this point in the campaign, there is wide recognition that some manner of accommodation with at least portions of the Taliban is necessary to stabilize the situation. The overall intent would be to degrade popular support for the Taliban and hive off reconcilable elements in order to further break apart the movement and make the ongoing security challenges more manageable. Ultimately, it is hoped, enough Taliban militants will be forced to the negotiating table to reduce the threat to the point where indigenous Afghan forces can keep a lid on the problem with minimal support.

Meanwhile, attempts at reaching out to the Taliban are now taking place on multiple tracks. In addition to efforts by the Karzai government, Washington has begun to support Saudi, Turkish and Pakistani efforts. At the moment, however, few Taliban groups seem to be in the mood to talk. At the very least they are playing hard to get, hinting at talks but maintaining the firm stance that full withdrawal of U.S. and ISAF forces is a precondition for negotiations.

The current U.S./NATO strategy faces several key challenges. For one thing, the Taliban are working on a completely different timeline than the United States, which — even separating itself from many of its anxious-to-withdraw NATO allies — is poised to begin drawing down forces in less than 18 months. While this is less of a fixed timetable than it appears (beginning to draw down from nearly 100,000 U.S. and nearly 40,000 ISAF troops in mid-2011 could still leave more than 100,000 troops in Afghanistan well into 2012), the Taliban are all too aware of Washington's limited commitment.

Then there are the intelligence issues:

- One of the inherent problems with the Vietnamization of a conflict is operational security and the reality that it is easy for insurgent groups to penetrate and compromise foreign efforts to build effective indigenous forces. In short, U.S./ISAF efforts with Afghan forces are relatively easy for the Taliban to compromise, while U.S./ISAF efforts to penetrate the Taliban are exceedingly difficult.

- U.S. Maj. Gen. Michael Flynn, the top intelligence officer in Afghanistan who is responsible for both ISAF and separate U.S. efforts, published a damning indictment of intelligence activity in the country last month and has moved to reorganize and refocus those efforts more on understanding the cultural terrain in which the United States and ISAF are operating. But while this shift will improve intelligence operations in the long run, the shake-up is taking place amid a surge of combat troops and ongoing offensive operations. Gen. David Petraeus, head of U.S. Central Command, and Gen. McChrystal have both made it clear that the United States lacks the sophisticated understanding of the various elements of the Taliban necessary to identify the potentially reconcilable elements. This is a key weakness in a strategy that ultimately requires such reconciliation (though it is unlikely to disrupt counterterrorism and the hunting of high-value targets).

The United States and ISAF are also struggling with information operations (IO), failing to effectively convey messages to and shape the perceptions of the Afghan people. Currently, the Taliban have the upper hand in terms of IO and have relatively little problem disseminating messages about U.S./ISAF activities and its own goals. The implication of this is that, in the contest over the hearts and minds of the Afghan people, the Taliban are winning the battle of perception.

The training of the ANA and ANP is also at issue. Due to attrition, tens of thousands of new recruits are necessary each year simply to maintain minimum numbers, much less add to the force. Goals for the size of the ANA and ANP are aggressive, but how quickly these goals can be achieved and the degree to which problems of infiltration can be managed — as well as the level of infiltration that can be tolerated while retaining reasonable effectiveness — all remain to be seen. In addition, loyalty to a central government has no cultural precedent in Afghanistan. The lack of a coherent national identity means that, while there are good reasons for young Afghan men to join up (a livelihood, tribal loyalty), there is no commitment to a national Afghan campaign. There are concerns that the Afghan security forces, left to their own devices, would simply devolve into militias along ethnic, tribal, political and ideological lines. Thus the sustainability of gains in the size and effectiveness of the ANA and ANP remains questionable.

This strategy also depends a great deal on the government of Afghan President Hamid Karzai, over which U.S. Ambassador Karl Eikenberry has expressed deep concern. The Karzai government is widely accused of rampant corruption and of having every intention of maintaining a heavy dependency on the United States. Doubts are often expressed about Karzai's intent and ability to be an effective partner in the military-political efforts now under way in his country.

While the United States has already made significant inroads against the Taliban in Helmand province, insurgents there are declining to fight and disappearing into the population. It is natural for an insurgency to fall back in the face of concentrated force and rise again when that force is removed, and the durability of these American gains could prove illusory. As Maj. Gen. Flynn's criticism demonstrates, the Pentagon is acutely aware of challenges it faces in Afghanistan. It is fair to say that the United States is pursuing the surge with its eyes open to inherent weaknesses and challenges. The question is: Can those challenges be overcome in a war-torn country with a long and proven history of insurgency?

The Meaning of Marjah
Feb. 16, 2010

On Feb. 13, some 6,000 U.S. Marines, soldiers and Afghan National Army (ANA) troops launched a sustained assault on the town of Marjah in Helmand province. Until this latest offensive, the U.S. and NATO effort in Afghanistan had been constrained by other considerations, most notably Iraq. Western forces viewed the

Afghan conflict as a matter of holding the line or pursuing targets of opportunity. But now, armed with larger forces and a new strategy, the war — the real war — has begun. The most recent offensive, dubbed Operation Moshtarak ("Moshtarak" is Dari for "together"), is the largest joint U.S./NATO-Afghan operation in history. It also is the first major offensive conducted by the first units deployed as part of the surge of 30,000 troops promised by U.S. President Barack Obama.

The United States originally entered Afghanistan in the aftermath of the 9/11 attacks. In those days of fear and fury, American goals could be simply stated: A non-state actor — al Qaeda — had attacked the American homeland and needed to be destroyed. Al Qaeda was based in Afghanistan at the invitation of a near-state actor — the Taliban, which at the time were Afghanistan's de facto governing force. Since the Taliban were unwilling to hand al Qaeda over, the United States attacked. By the end of the year, al Qaeda had relocated to neighboring Pakistan and the Taliban retreated into the arid, mountainous countryside in their southern heartland and began waging a guerrilla conflict. In time, American attention became split between searching for al Qaeda and clashing with the Taliban over control of Afghanistan.

But from the earliest days following 9/11, the White House was eyeing Iraq, and with the Taliban having largely declined combat in the initial invasion, the path seemed clear. The U.S. military and diplomatic focus was shifted, and as the years wore on, the conflict absorbed more and more U.S. troops, even as other issues — a resurgent Russia and a defiant Iran — began to demand American attention. All of this and more consumed American bandwidth, and the Afghan conflict melted into the background. The United States maintained its Afghan force in what could accurately be described as a holding action as the bulk of its forces operated elsewhere. That has more or less been the state of affairs for eight years.

That has changed with the series of offensive operations that most recently culminated at Marjah. Why Marjah? The key is the geography of Afghanistan and the nature of the conflict itself. Most of Afghanistan is perfect for a guerrilla war. Much of the country is mountainous, encouraging local identities and militias, as well as complicating the task of any foreign military force. The country's aridity discourages dense population centers (see map on page 33), making it very easy for irregular combatants to melt into the countryside. Afghanistan lacks navigable rivers or ports, drastically reducing the region's likelihood of developing commerce. No commerce to tax means fewer resources to fund a meaningful government or military and encourages the smuggling of every good imaginable — and that smuggling provides the perfect funding for guerrillas.

Rooting out insurgents is no simple task. It requires three things:

- Massively superior numbers so that occupiers can limit the zones to which the insurgents have easy access.

- The support of the locals in order to limit the places that the guerillas can disappear into.

- Superior intelligence so that the fight can be consistently taken to the insurgents rather than vice versa.

Without those three things — and American-led forces in Afghanistan lack all three — the insurgents can simply take the fight to the occupiers, retreat to rearm and regroup and return again shortly thereafter.

But the insurgents hardly hold all the cards. Guerrilla forces are by their very nature irregular. Their capacity to organize and strike is quite limited, and while they can turn a region into a hellish morass for an opponent, they have great difficulty holding territory — particularly territory that a regular force chooses to contest. Should they mass into a force that could achieve a major battlefield victory, a regular force — which is by definition better-funded, -trained, -organized and -armed — will almost always smash the irregulars. Hence, the default guerrilla tactic is to attrit and harass the occupier into giving up and going home. The guerrillas always decline combat in the face of a superior military force only to come back and fight at a time and

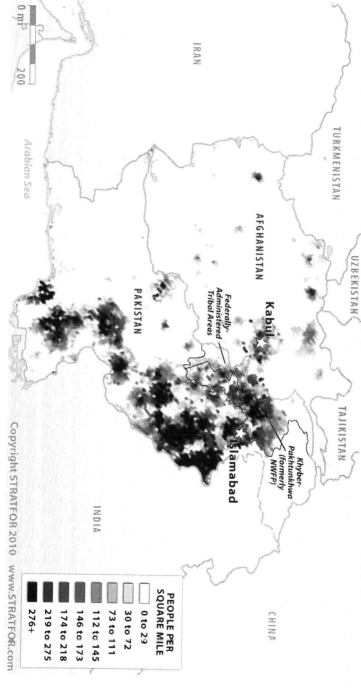

AFGHANISTAN AND PAKISTAN POPULATION DENSITY

TURKMENISTAN

UZBEKISTAN

TAJIKISTAN

CHINA

IRAN

AFGHANISTAN

PAKISTAN

INDIA

Arabian Sea

Kabul

Islamabad

Federally-
Administered
Tribal Areas

Khyber-
Pakhtunkhwa
(formerly
NWFP)

0 mi   200

Copyright STRATFOR 2010   www.STRATFOR.com

PEOPLE PER
SQUARE MILE

0 to 29
30 to 72
73 to 111
112 to 145
146 to 173
174 to 218
219 to 275
276+

place of their choosing. Time is always on the guerrilla's side if the regular force is not a local one.

But while the guerrillas don't require basing locations that are as large or as formalized as those required by regular forces, they are still bound by basic economics. They need resources — money, men and weapons — to operate. The larger their basing locations are, the better economies of scale they can achieve and the more effectively they can fight their war.

Marjah is perhaps the quintessential example of a good location from which to base. It is in a region sympathetic to the Taliban; Helmand province is part of the Taliban's heartland. Marjah is very close to Kandahar, Afghanistan's second-largest city, the religious center of the local brand of Islam, the birthplace of the Taliban, and due to the presence of American forces, an excellent target. Helmand alone produces more heroin than any country on the planet, and Marjah is at the center of that trade. By some estimates, this center alone supplies the Taliban with a monthly income of $200,000. And it is defensible: The farmland is crisscrossed with irrigation canals and dotted with mud-brick compounds — and, given time to prepare, a veritable plague of improvised explosive devices.

Simply put, regardless of the Taliban's strategic or tactical goals, Marjah is a critical node in their operations.

The American Strategy

Though operations have approached Marjah in the past, it has not been something NATO's International Security Assistance Force (ISAF) ever has tried to hold. The British, Canadian and Danish troops holding the line in the country's restive south had their hands full enough. Despite Marjah's importance to the Taliban, ISAF forces were too few to engage the Taliban everywhere (and they remain as such). But American priorities started changing about two years ago. The surge of forces into Iraq changed the position of many a player in the country. Those changes allowed a reshaping of the Iraq conflict that laid the groundwork for the current "stability" and American withdrawal. At the same time in Afghanistan, the Taliban began to resurge in a big way. Since then the Bush and then Obama administrations have inched toward applying a similar strategy to Afghanistan, a strategy that focuses less on battlefield success and more on altering the parameters of the country itself.

As the Obama administration's strategy has begun to take shape, it has started thinking about endgames. A decades-long occupation and pacification of Afghanistan is simply not in the cards. A withdrawal is, but only a withdrawal where the security free-for-all that allowed al Qaeda to thrive will not return. And this is where Marjah comes in.

Denying the Taliban control of poppy farming communities like Marjah and the key population centers along the Helmand River Valley — and areas like them around the country — is the first goal of the American strategy. The fewer key population centers the Taliban can count on, the more dispersed — and militarily inefficient — their forces will be. This will hardly destroy the Taliban, but destruction isn't the goal. The Taliban are not simply a militant Islamist force. At times they are a flag of convenience for businessmen or thugs; they can even be, simply, the least-bad alternative for villagers desperate for basic security and civil services. In many parts of Afghanistan, the Taliban are not only pervasive but also the sole option for governance and civil authority.

So destruction of what is in essence part of the local cultural and political fabric is not an American goal. Instead, the goal is to prevent the Taliban from mounting large-scale operations that could overwhelm any particular location. Remember, the Americans do not wish to pacify Afghanistan; the Americans wish to leave Afghanistan in a form that will not cause the United States severe problems down the road. In effect, achieving the first goal simply aims to shape the ground for a shot at achieving the second.

That second goal is to establish a domestic authority that can stand up to the Taliban in the long run. Most of the surge of forces into Afghanistan is not designed to battle the Taliban now but to secure the population and train the Afghan security forces to battle the Taliban later. To do this, the Taliban must be weak enough in a formal military sense to be unable to launch massive or coordinated attacks. Capturing key population centers along the Helmand River Valley is the first step in a strategy designed to create the breathing room necessary to create a replacement force, preferably a replacement force that provides Afghans with a viable alternative to the Taliban.

That is no small task. In recent years, in places where the official government has been corrupt, inept or defunct, the Taliban have in many cases stepped in to provide basic governance and civil authority. And this is why even the Americans are publicly considering with holding talks with certain factions of the Taliban in hopes that at least some of the fighters can be dissuaded from battling the Americans (assisting with the first goal) and perhaps persuaded to join the nascent Afghan government (assisting with the second).

The bottom line is that this battle does not mark the turning of the tide of the war. Instead, it is part of the application of a new strategy that accurately takes into account Afghanistan's geography and all the weaknesses and challenges that geography poses. Marjah marks the first time the United States has applied a plan not to hold the line, but actually to reshape the country. We are not saying that the strategy will bear fruit. Afghanistan is a corrupt mess populated by citizens who are far more comfortable thinking and acting locally and tribally than nationally. In such a place indigenous guerrillas will always hold the advantage. No one has ever attempted this sort of national restructuring in Afghanistan, and the Americans are attempting to do so in a short period on a shoestring budget.

At the time of this writing, this first step appears to be going well for American-NATO-Afghan forces. Casualties have been light and most of Marjah already has been secured. But do not read this as a massive battlefield success. The assault required weeks of obvious preparation, and very few Taliban fighters chose to remain and contest the territory against the more numerous and better-armed attackers. The American challenge lies not so much in assaulting or capturing Marjah but in continuing to deny it to the Taliban. If the Americans cannot actually hold places like Marjah, then they are simply engaging in an exhausting and reactive strategy of chasing a dispersed and mobile target.

A "government-in-a-box" of civilian administrators is already poised to move into Marjah to step into the vacuum left by the Taliban. We obviously have major doubts about how effective this box government can be at building up civil authority in a town that has been governed by the Taliban for most of the last decade. Yet what happens in Marjah and places like it in the coming months will be the foundation upon which the success or failure of this effort will be built. But assessing that process is simply impossible, because the only measure that matters cannot be judged until the Afghans are left to themselves.

The Battle for the Ring Road
March 16, 2010

The transportation infrastructure in Afghanistan is notoriously abysmal. Roads are primitive and few, and regional rail networks do not even enter the country. And the U.S./NATO military machine is notoriously heavy and fuel-intensive, which makes for a mountain of logistical challenges. Although a northern distribution route has opened up, operations are sustained by an army of civilian Pakistani truck drivers who transport most of the supplies — especially fuel — for the U.S./NATO military effort.

At the heart of what passes for a road network in Afghanistan is Highway 1, or the "Ring Road" (also known as the Garland Highway), which is the central artery connecting the country's four main population centers — Mazar-i-Sharif, Kabul, Kandahar and Herat. The roadway, parts of it unpaved, has existed in one form or another since before the Soviet invasion, but only since about 2003 have efforts been made to improve and complete it. The section from Leman and Maimana is still under construction, and a stretch from

Kabul to Kandahar has had to be repaired due to neglect and damage from improvised explosive devices (IEDs).

The U.S. Agency for International Development and the Asian Development Bank have spent some $2.5 billion on the project, but efforts have been hampered by attacks, kidnappings and other forms of intimidation by insurgents and common criminals. Between 2003 and 2008, more than 160 contractors were killed working on the southern arch from Kabul to Herat in a still-ongoing effort to complete the nearly 2,000-mile-long loop. Companies of police officers have had to be organized and dispatched at great expense to secure construction efforts.

At the same time, International Security Assistance Force (ISAF) military and civilian development efforts have identified 80 key districts as priorities. Governance, development and security programs are in the process of being implemented in these districts, most of which are located on or near the Ring Road.

This is no accident. Not only is the highway important logistically, but U.S. estimates put two-thirds of the Afghan population within about 30 miles of the loop. While the Ring Road is of pivotal importance in sustaining surge operations, it is also crucial in facilitating the current U.S. population-centric strategy, which is an economy-of-force move to focus efforts on key population centers.

But because almost everything in Afghanistan is an economy-of-force effort, not all sections of the Ring Road can be heavily protected. Some 800 Romanian troops are reportedly responsible for securing more than 100 miles of roadway through Zabul province, part of the critical link between Kabul and Kandahar. And because there are so few roads in Afghanistan, the ones that are heavily relied upon are easy targets for insurgents and IEDs.

The United States is working to deploy better off-road vehicles into the country to provide more logistical and tactical flexibility. But the Ring Road is also about national development and commerce. Afghanistan's economy is minimal, but part of the U.S. strategy is to reshape public perceptions in the key population centers connected by the roadway. If the Ring Road is open and safe to travel, it will

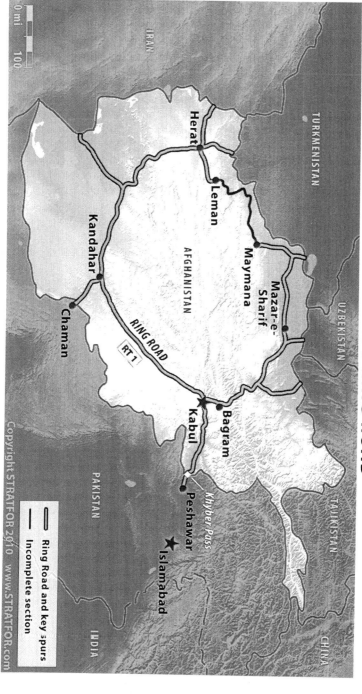

AFGHANISTAN'S RING ROAD

Ring Road and key spurs
Incomplete section

greatly facilitate the development of economic and governmental links between and among Kabul and the other key cities. If it is not, the effort will be greatly hindered.

Another consideration, of course, is history. Foreign powers have often tried to rule Afghanistan from the top down, to little avail. The political, demographic, ethnic and tribal realities of Afghanistan mean that the country is best ruled from the bottom up. The U.S./NATO effort is now focused on the district level, more of a bottom-up approach, but whether this strategy can succeed in engaging people at the grassroots level in any meaningful way — especially on the 18-month timetable that ISAF chief Gen. Stanley McChrystal is working within — is anything but certain. And the success of the overall war strategy will depend on a lot more than just the safety of the Ring Road.

But both the roadway and the patchwork of priority districts that lie along or near it will bear considerable watching as the ISAF strategy continues to unfold.

Another Round in the IED Game
March 31, 2010

Though it has long been associated most with the war in Iraq, the improvised explosive device (IED) has become the No. 1 killer of Western troops now driving the roads and plodding through the poppy fields of Afghanistan. Since 2004, IED fatalities for coalition military forces there have roughly doubled every year, with deaths so far in 2010 already having reached the 2007 total.

Thus far, the Afghan IED has been fairly distinct from the Iraqi variety. Neither country has any shortage of loose military hardware, but conventional military ordnance like large artillery shells has long been more prevalent in Iraq, due to the country's history of having a large standing army organized and equipped broadly along Soviet lines. The Iraqi military also stockpiled weapons in hidden caches ahead of the U.S. invasion, specifically for a protracted guerrilla campaign. The Iraqi IED also came to be characterized by a particularly deadly variety known as an explosively formed projectile (EFP), which was supplied by Iran. The EFP is constructed with concave copper disks, and the explosion shapes the copper into a molten penetrator that can punch through heavy armor.

In Afghanistan, however, the heart of most IEDs is fertilizer, generally ammonium nitrate or potassium chloride, both of which have been readily available in the agrarian country. The former is far more powerful and has consequently been banned. Military-grade high explosives also detonate with a much higher velocity than devices based on fertilizer. And while IEDs in Iraq often used sophisticated command-detonation devices (which made U.S. jamming technology crucial as a countermeasure), IEDs in Afghanistan often use crude triggers such as pressure plates. Compared to Iraqi IEDs, Afghan devices also frequently have less metal, which makes them more difficult to find with traditional hand-held mine detectors. Indeed, modern versions of the old-fashioned mine roller, typically mounted in front of a mine-resistant ambush-protected (MRAP) vehicle built around a V-shaped hull designed to better withstand IEDs, are increasingly in demand in Afghanistan. K-9 units with explosive-detecting dogs also are reportedly being deployed more widely at the battalion level.

But the real issue is this back-and-forth game of tactics and countertactics that characterizes the IED battle. STRATFOR has long argued that the bombmaking techniques honed over the years in Iraq will proliferate more widely — Afghanistan being only one destination. And while many a bombmaker was killed or captured in Iraq during the high-intensity special operations forces raids that took place behind the scenes during the 2007 surge, others have begun to gravitate to places like Afghanistan, where their presence has contributed to the uptick in IED use. The tools at their disposal may be different to some extent, but the core expertise is what matters. With the right level of experience and skill, bombmakers can improvise and innovate, which speeds up the turnaround of new, deadlier designs.

In addition, Iran has reportedly been training Taliban fighters in IED fabrication and is turning its attention toward Afghanistan. Whether EFPs begin to turn up there in a big way remains to be seen, but they are not particularly complex devices when the right raw materials are available. The bottom line is that the regional focus — not only of Iran but also of countries like Russia and India — is increasingly shifting from Iraq to Afghanistan, which may lead to more interference in the U.S./NATO effort from beyond Afghanistan's borders.

At the same time, the International Security Assistance Force (ISAF) is working hard to counter the growing IED threat. Years of battling IEDs in Iraq have helped the United States hone its ability to quickly evaluate emerging IED trends and provide effective countermeasures. In Afghanistan, the ban on ammonium nitrate can hardly be effectively enforced, but it is certainly putting a pinch on an essential bombmaking material. And although the Taliban have begun to hit back in Helmand province, they are also feeling the loss of a key logistical hub in Marjah, where there are reports that bombmaking material has become increasingly scarce. There are also reports that more than half of the IEDs in Marjah are being found before they explode — staying "left of boom" in grunt parlance — due to evolving American tactics and techniques. And the deployment of MRAP all-terrain vehicles — more mobile and suitable for Afghanistan's rugged terrain than the cumbersome MRAPs introduced in Iraq — means that more troops will have a safer means of transport, though dismounted foot patrols will continue to be of central importance.

Still, because it has proved so effective, the deployment of IEDs will remain a key Taliban tactic, and they will continue to evolve their methods in response to U.S. countermeasures. With IEDs, this back-and-forth tactical evolution can come in particularly rapid cycles, with bombmakers rapidly learning from their successes and failures while American forensic teams try to identify and dissect the latest threat and devise an effective response. With more and more U.S. and allied troops surging into the country, just how this balance plays out and which side retains the edge will warrant close scrutiny. And the fact remains that, as in Iraq, the use of IEDs may be the deadliest insurgent tactic in Afghanistan, but it has yet to significantly impede ISAF operations.

CHAPTER 2: AFGHANISTAN AND THE TALIBAN

The Nature of the Insurgency
June 1, 2009

The United States is losing in Afghanistan because it is not winning. The Taliban are winning in Afghanistan because they are not losing. This is the reality of insurgent warfare. A local insurgent is more invested in the struggle and is working on a much longer timeline than an occupying foreign soldier. Every year that U.S. and NATO commanders do not show progress in Afghanistan, the investment of lives and resources becomes harder to justify at home. Public support erodes. Even without more pressing concerns elsewhere, democracies tend to have short attention spans.

At the present time, defense budgets across the developed world — like national coffers in general — are feeling the pinch of the global financial crisis. Meanwhile, the resurgence of Russia's power and influence along its periphery continues apace. The state of the current U.S./NATO Afghanistan campaign is not simply a matter of eroding public opinion, it is also a matter of immense opportunity costs due to mounting economic and geopolitical challenges elsewhere.

This reality plays into the hands of the insurgents. In any guerrilla struggle, the local populace is vulnerable to the violence and very sensitive to subtle shifts in power at the local level. As long as the foreign occupier's resolve continues to erode (as it almost inevitably does) or is made to appear to erode (by the insurgents), the insurgents maintain the upper hand. If the occupying power is perceived as a temporary reality for the local populace and the insurgents are an enduring reality, then the incentive for the locals — at the very least — is to not oppose the insurgents directly enough to incur their wrath when the occupying power leaves. For those who seek to benefit from the largesse and status that cooperation with the occupying power can provide, the enduring fear is the departure of that power before a decisive victory can be made against the insurgents — or before adequate security can be provided by an indigenous government army.

Let us apply this dynamic to the current situation in Afghanistan. In much of the extremely rugged, rural and sparsely populated country, a sustained presence by the U.S./NATO and the Taliban alike is not possible. No one is in clear control in most parts of the country. The strength of the tribal power structure was systematically undermined by the communists long before the actual Soviet invasion at the end of 1979. The power structure that remains is nowhere near as strong or as uniform as, say, that of the Sunni tribes in Anbar province in Iraq (one important reason why replicating the Iraq counterinsurgency in Afghanistan is not possible). Indeed, it is difficult to overstate the unique complexity of the ethnic, linguistic and tribal disparities in Afghanistan.

The challenge for each side in the current Afghan war is to become more of a sustained presence than the other. "Holding" territory is not possible in the traditional sense, with so few troops and hard-line insurgent fighters involved, so a village can be "pro-NATO" one day and "pro-Taliban" the next, depending on who happens to be moving through the area. But even village and tribal leaders who do work with the West are extremely hesitant to burn any bridges with the Taliban, lest U.S./NATO forces withdraw before defeating the insurgents and before developing a sufficient replacement force of Afghan nationals.

Today, the two primary sources of power in Afghanistan are the gun and the Koran — brute force and religious credibility. The Taliban purport to base their power on both, while the United States and NATO are often derided for wielding only the former — and clumsily at that. Many Afghans believe that too many innocent civilians have been killed in too many indiscriminate airstrikes.

So it comes as little surprise that popular support for the Taliban is on the rise in more and more parts of Afghanistan, and that this support is becoming increasingly entrenched. For years, U.S. attention has been distracted and military power absorbed in Iraq. Meanwhile, a limited U.S./NATO presence and a lack of opposition in Afghanistan have allowed various elements of the Taliban to make significant inroads. This resurgence is also due to clandestine support from Pakistan's army and Inter-Services Intelligence (ISI) directorate, as well as proximity to the mountainous and lawless Pakistani border area, which serves as a Taliban sanctuary.

But the Taliban still have not coalesced to the point where they can eject U.S. or NATO forces from Afghanistan. Far from a monolithic movement, the term "Taliban" encompasses everything from the old hard-liners of the pre-9/11 Afghan regime to small groups that adopt the name as a "flag of convenience," be they Islamists devoted to a local cause or criminals wanting to obscure their true objectives. Some Taliban elements in Pakistan are waging their own insurrection against Islamabad. (The multifaceted and often confusing character of the Taliban "movement" actually creates a layer of protection around it. The United States has admitted that it does not have the nuanced understanding of the Taliban's composition needed to identify potential moderates who can be split off from the hard-liners.)

Any "revolutionary" or insurgent force usually has two enemies: the foreign occupying or indigenous government power it is trying to defeat, and other revolutionary entities with which it is competing. While making inroads against the former, the Taliban have not yet resolved the issue of the latter. It is not so much that various insurgent groups with distinctly different ideologies are in direct competition with each other; the problem for the Taliban, reflecting the rough reality that the country's mountainous and rugged terrain imposes on its people, is the disparate nature of the movement itself.

In order to precipitate a U.S./NATO withdrawal in the years ahead, the Taliban must do better in consolidating their power. No doubt they currently have the upper hand, but their strategic and tactical advantages will only go so far. They may be enough to prevent the United States and NATO from winning, but they will not accelerate the timeline for a Taliban victory. To do this, the Taliban must move beyond current guerrilla tactics and find ways to function as a more coherent and coordinated fighting force.

The bottom line is that neither side in the struggle in Afghanistan is currently operating at its full potential.

To Grow an Insurgency

The main benefits of waging an insurgency usually boil down to the following: insurgents operate in squad- to platoon-sized elements, have light or nonexistent logistical tails, are largely able to live off the land or the local populace, can support themselves by seizing weapons and ammunition from weak local police and isolated outposts and can disperse and blend into the environment whenever they confront larger and more powerful conventional forces. In Afghanistan, the chief insurgent challenge is that reasonably well-defended U.S./NATO positions have no problem fending off units of that size. In the evolution of an insurgency, we call this stage-one warfare, and Taliban operations by and large continue to be characterized as such.

In stage-two warfare, insurgents operate in larger formations — first independent companies of roughly 100 or so fighters, and later battalions of several hundred or more. Although still relatively small and flexible, these units require more in terms of logistics, especially as they begin to employ heavier, more supply-intensive weaponry like crew-served machine guns and mortars, and they are too large to simply disperse the moment contact with the enemy is made. The challenges include not only logistics but also battlefield communications (everything from bugles and whistles to cell phones and secure tactical radios) as the unit becomes too large for a single leader to manage or visually keep track of from one position.

In stage-three warfare, the insurgent force has become, for all practical purposes, a conventional army operating in regiments and divisions (units, say, consisting of 1,000 or more troops). These units are large enough to bring artillery to bear but must be able to provide a steady flow of ammunition. Forces of this size are an immense logistical challenge and, once massed, cannot quickly be dispersed, which makes them vulnerable to superior firepower.

The culmination of this evolution is exemplified by the battle of Dien Bien Phu in a highland valley in northwestern Vietnam in 1954. The Viet Minh, which began as a nationalist guerrilla group fighting the Japanese during World War II, massed multiple divisions and brought artillery to bear against a French military position considered impregnable. The battle lasted two months and saw the French position overrun. More than 2,000 French soldiers were killed, more than twice that many wounded and more than 10,000 captured. The devastating defeat was quickly followed by the French withdrawal from Indochina after an eight-year counterinsurgency.

The Taliban Today

In describing this progression from stage one to stage three, we are not necessarily suggesting that the Taliban will develop into a conventional force, or that a stage-three capability is necessary to win in Afghanistan. Not every insurgency that achieves victory does so by evolving into the kind of national-level conventional resistance made legendary by the Viet Minh.

Indeed, artillery was not necessary to expel the Soviet Red Army from Afghanistan in the 1980s; that force faced and failed to overcome many of the same challenges that have repelled invaders for centuries and confront the United States and NATO today. But in monitoring the progress of the Taliban as a fighting force, it is important to look beyond estimates of "controlled" territory to the way the

Taliban fight, command, consolidate and organize disparate groups into a more coherent resistance.

The Taliban first rose to power in the aftermath of the Soviet occupation of Afghanistan and before 9/11. They were not the ones to kick out the Red Army, however. That was the mujahideen, with the support of Pakistan, Saudi Arabia and the United States. The Taliban emerged from the anarchy that followed the fall of Afghanistan's communist government, also at the hands of the mujahideen, in 1992. In the intra-Islamist civil war that ensued, the Taliban were able to establish security in the southern part of the country, winning over a local Pashtun populace and assorted minorities that had grown weary of war.

This impressed Pakistan, which switched its support from the splintered mujahideen to the Taliban, which appeared to be on a roll. By 1996, the Taliban, also supported by Saudi Arabia and the United Arab Emirates, were in power in Kabul. Then came 9/11. While the Taliban did, for a time, achieve a kind of stage-two status as a fighting force, they have never had the kind of superpower support the Viet Minh and North Vietnamese received from the Soviet Union during the French and American wars in Vietnam, or that the mujahideen received from the United States during the Soviet occupation of Afghanistan.

But elements of the Taliban continue to enjoy patronage from within the Pakistani army and intelligence apparatus, as well as continued funding from wealthy patrons in the Persian Gulf states. The Pakistani support underscores the most important of resources for an effective insurgency (or counterinsurgency): intelligence. With it, the Taliban can obtain accurate and actionable information on competing insurgent groups in order to build a wider and more concerted campaign. They can also identify targets, adjust tactics and exploit the weaknesses of opposing conventional forces. The Taliban openly tout their ties and support from within the Afghan security forces. (Indeed, a significant portion of the Taliban's weapons and ammunition can be traced back to shipments that were made to the Afghan government and distributed to its police agencies and military units.)

Moreover, while external support of the Taliban may not be as impressive as the support the mujahideen enjoyed in the 1980s, the Karzai government in Afghanistan is far weaker than the communist regime in Kabul that the mujahideen took down. In addition, as a seven-party alliance with significant internal tensions, the mujahideen were even more disjointed than the Taliban. Indeed, the core Taliban today are much more homogeneous than the mujahideen were in the 1980s. The Taliban are the pre-eminent Pashtun power, and the Pashtuns are the single largest ethnic group in Afghanistan. In addition, the leadership of Taliban chief Mullah Omar is unchallenged — he has no equal who could hope to rise and meaningfully compete for control of the movement.

While the Taliban continue to exist squarely in stage-one combat, the movement is increasingly becoming the established, lasting reality for much of the country's rural population. For ambitious warlords, joining the Taliban movement offers legitimacy and a local fiefdom with wider recognition. For the remainder of the population, the Taliban are increasingly perceived as the inescapable power that will govern when the United States and NATO begin to draw down.

On the other hand, the Taliban's ability to earn the loyalty of disparate groups, coordinate their actions and command them effectively remains to be seen. Monitoring changes in the way the Taliban communicate — across the country and across the battlefield — will say much about their ability to bring power to bear in a coherent, coordinated and conclusive way.

The Taliban in Afghanistan: An Assessment
Sept. 28, 2009

The Taliban are a direct product of the intra-Islamist civil war that erupted following the fall of the Afghan Marxist regime in 1992, only three years after the withdrawal of Soviet forces. Dating back to

51

the 1960s, the Soviet-allied communist party in Afghanistan sought to undermine the local tribal structure: It wanted to gain power via central control. This strategy was extremely disruptive and resulted in a deterioration of order and the evisceration of the traditional tribal ethnic system of relations. But these efforts could not dislodge regional and local warlords, who continued to fight among themselves for territorial control with little regard for civilians, long the modus operandi in Afghanistan.

After the Islamist uprising against the communist takeover and the subsequent entry of Soviet troops into the country in 1979, disparate Afghan factions united under the banner of Islam, aided by the then-Islamist-leaning regime in neighboring Pakistan, which was backed by the United States and Saudi Arabia. In terms of the Taliban movement, Pakistan was the most influential, but Saudi Arabia and the United Arab Emirates were also involved — mostly through financial support. The Saudis had political and religious ties as well.

During this time, madrassas (Islamic seminaries) in Pakistan became incubators, drawing young, mostly ethnic Pashtuns who would in turn facilitate the later rise of the Taliban in the early to mid-1990s in the wake of the decline of the mujahedeen factions. The madrassas allowed war orphans and male youth among the displaced refugees to study in Pakistan while Afghanistan experienced a brutal civil war. These Afghans were taught a particularly ultraconservative brand of Islam (and the able-bodied among them received training in guerrilla tactics), with the idea that when they returned to Afghanistan, Pakistan would be able to control them and thereby maintain a powerful lever over its volatile and often unpredictable neighbor.

These radicalized fighters, many of whom considered themselves devoted students of Islam, labeled themselves "Taliban," which comes from the word for student — "Talib" — in several regional languages, with Taliban being the plural form in Pashto. The Taliban restored some sense of law and order by enforcing their own austere brand of Shariah in areas where local warlords previously ruled as they pleased — often to the detriment of civilians. The Taliban, arresting and executing offending warlords, avenged injustices such as rape, murder and theft. As a result, the Taliban won support from the locals by providing a greater sense of security and justice.

By the mid-1990s, the Taliban had become more cohesive under their nominal leader from Kandahar, Mullah Mohammad Omar. The Taliban gained prominence as a faction in 1994 when they were able to impose order amid chaos in the Kandahar region. By 1996, Taliban forces had entered Kabul, overthrown then-President Burhanuddin Rabbani and claimed control, renaming the country "The Islamic Emirate of Afghanistan." Omar was named the leader of the country but remained in Kandahar. It was during this rise to power that outside forces began partnering with the Taliban — namely al Qaeda — emphasizing their common radical Islamist ideology, but ultimately putting the Taliban in unsavory company. Pakistan and al Qaeda competed for influence over the Taliban, with Pakistan seeking to use them as leverage in Afghanistan and al Qaeda wanting to use the Taliban's control over Afghanistan to spread their power throughout the Islamic world.

During their rule, the Taliban attempted to rid Afghanistan of any Western influences that had crept in, such as Western clothing, movies, music, schools and political ideologies. The proxy forces of the Pakistanis were now essentially governing the state, providing Pakistan with a tremendous amount of influence in Afghanistan and, consequently, a very secure western border, which allowed Pakistan to focus on India to the east.

But this situation did not last long. Al Qaeda's influence was on the upswing in Afghanistan, from which it staged the 9/11 attacks. As a result, and after the refusal of the Taliban regime to disassociate itself from al Qaeda, the Afghan jihadist group was forced out of power by U.S. forces in late 2001. (The United States implicated the Taliban in providing sanctuary to al Qaeda.) Instead of fighting against conventionally superior U.S. and NATO forces, the Taliban retreated into their traditional rural support bases in the south and east. In other words, despite both claims and perceptions of a quick

U.S. victory in Afghanistan in 2002, the Taliban largely declined to fight.

In many ways, there was no real interregnum between the fall of the regime and the insurgency. The West's earliest attempts to talk to the Taliban occurred in 2003, a sign that the West viewed the Taliban as a force that had not been defeated and was capable of staging a comeback. In the early days, the West's strategy was to eliminate the Taliban as a fighting force, but they were never successful, due to adverse geography, a lack of Western forces and a shifting of focus to Iraq in 2003. More important, the fight to control the Pashtun areas turned into a fight to prevent a resurgent Taliban. The U.S. focus on the insurgency in Iraq allowed the Taliban to galvanize and regroup, and by 2005 it was clear that they were rebounding. Since 2006, the Taliban insurgency has gained momentum to the point that U.S. Army Gen. David Petraeus commented in April that foreign forces in Afghanistan are dealing with an "industrial strength" insurgency.

The Current Status of the Taliban

Despite their removal from power in Kabul, the Taliban continue to be the most powerful indigenous force in Afghanistan. Unlike the Afghan National Army or the Afghan National Police, which are built around the idea that Afghanistan can be centrally controlled, the Taliban have a much looser command structure that functions on regional and local levels. Various Taliban commanders have attempted to control the movement and call it their own, but the disjointedness of Taliban units means that each commander enjoys independence and ultimately controls his own men. The Afghan Taliban should also not be confused with the Tehrik-i-Taliban Pakistan (TTP), the main Pakistani Taliban rebel coalition. The TTP is an indigenous movement, and while it cooperates with the Afghan Taliban and shares similar objectives, the two groups are independent.

The closest the Afghan Taliban have to a central leader is Omar, who has no coequal. He has recently issued orders in an attempt to consolidate the disparate forces in various regions. However, such orders are not always followed, largely because the malleable and semi-autonomous command structure allows the Taliban to be much more in tune with the structural realities of operating in Afghanistan than the Afghan forces created by the U.S.-led International Security Assistance Force (ISAF) or the U.S. and ISAF forces themselves.

Though a loose command and control structure prevents the enemy from targeting any central nerve center that would significantly disrupt the group's existence, the nebulous structure of the Taliban also prevents them from being a single, coherent force with a single, coherent mission. The Taliban fighting force is far from uniform. Fighters range from young locals who are either fighting for ideological reasons or are forced by circumstances to fight with the Taliban, to hardened, well-trained veterans of the Soviet war in the 1980s, to foreigners who have come to Afghanistan to cut their teeth fighting Western forces and contribute their assistance to re-establishing the "Islamic" emirate.

This also leads to variable objectives. On the most basic level, the desire to drive out foreign forces from the area and control it for themselves is a sentiment that appeals to every Taliban fighter and many Afghan civilians. The Taliban know that foreigners have never been able to impose order on the country and that it is only a matter of time before foreign forces leave, which is when the Taliban — being the single-most organized militia — could have the opportunity to restore their lost "emirate." The presence of foreign soldiers restricts their ability to administer self rule, but it also is what keeps the Taliban somewhat united.

However, the Afghan national identity is easily trumped by subnational ones. While there is consensus on the idea of opposing foreign militaries, agreement becomes more tenuous when it comes to Afghan security forces. Tribal and ethnic identities tend to trump any national identity, meaning that the ethnic Balochis in the south are unlikely to support the presence of an ethnic Pashtun military unit from Kabul in their home village.

Taliban forces across Afghanistan share one goal: removing the foreign military presence. And these militants know that direct confrontation with foreign military forces typically ends poorly for them, since, given enough time, foreign forces can muster far superior firepower. For this reason, the Taliban rely heavily on indirect fire and improvised explosive devices (IEDs), which avoid putting Taliban fighters directly in harm's way. When Taliban fighters do confront military forces directly, it is generally (though not universally) in the form of hit-and-run ambushes (often supported by heavy machine guns and mortars) that seek to inflict damage through surprise, not overwhelming force.

Rough terrain and meager transportation infrastructure restrict mobility in Afghanistan, which limits the routes that ground convoys can take, especially in outlying areas where the Taliban enjoy more freedom to operate. This makes routes predictable and creates more choke points where IEDs can be placed, which have caused the most deaths for U.S. and NATO forces in Afghanistan.

These tactics do not always inflict damage on foreign forces and are often unsuccessful, but their model is low-risk, cheap and very sustainable. Meanwhile, as Taliban forces inflict casualties against foreign forces, the overall campaign becomes harder to sustain for Western governments.

Additionally, suicide bombings and suicide vehicle-borne impro-vised explosive devices (VBIEDs) are on the rise in areas like Kabul. However, various elements of the Taliban (as well as many foreign jihadists) have not proved to be able to use these tactics as effectively as Iraqi or Pakistani militants. This is because the Afghan Taliban have much more experience using guerrilla tactics, fighting as small, armed units, than using terrorist tactics such as VBIEDs and suicide bombings. VBIEDs are hardly indigenous to Afghanistan and did not become common until around 2005-06, well after they had become common in Iraq. As militants migrated from different jihadist theaters and shared information, tactics spread to Afghanistan. There was also an effort by al Qaeda to impart its tactics to the Taliban. But there is a learning curve for perfecting the construction of these weapons and the tactical expertise to employ them. While the Taliban have not been as proficient as some of their contemporaries, their capability could be improving.

It remains to be seen what kind of implications the collateral damage that these attacks cause will have on the popular perception of the movement. One clear implication of killing civilians is that it undermines local support for the Taliban, which is why Omar has sought to limit the use of suicide bombings (which Afghans have traditionally abhorred). But the continued employment of such tactics against Afghan and Western security forces can be expected.

However, areas where the Taliban conduct attacks should not be confused with areas that the Taliban control. Attacks certainly indicate a Taliban presence, but the Taliban would not necessarily need to conduct sustained attacks in an area where they did not feel threatened. The issue of controlling territory is, in fact, much more complex. Many mainstream publications have attempted to calculate what percentage of Afghanistan is under Taliban "control" or where the Taliban have influence. But these terms are misleading and need to be properly defined to understand the reality of the insurgency and its grip on the country.

'Controlling' Afghanistan

Western military forces and the Taliban have pursued different strategies to control territory in Afghanistan. Foreign forces have used the model of controlling the national capital and projecting power into the provinces. For them, Kabul is the main objective, with other major cities and provincial capitals being the secondary objective, followed by district capitals and smaller towns as the third objective. Foreign forces tend to hold urban areas because they are crucial to maintaining supply chains and meeting heavier logistical needs, and because such areas are deemed necessary to carry out a more centralized conception of national governance. Holding urban areas and roads allows foreign forces to expand farther into the rural areas where, conversely, the Taliban derive their power.

The Taliban implement almost the exact opposite model. The Taliban employ decentralized control with a much lighter logistical footprint. The Taliban begin at the local level, in isolated villages and towns, so that they can pressure district-level capitals. This scheme, which comes naturally to the Taliban, is much more in line with the underlying realities of Afghanistan.

Both sides have managed to prevent the other from gaining any real control over the country. By holding district and provincial capitals, foreign forces deny the Taliban formal control. By entrenching themselves in the countryside, the Taliban simply survive — and can afford to wait for their opportunity.

Few areas of the country are secure for Taliban, foreign or Afghan forces — or civilians — indicating that no side has absolute control over territory. What STRATFOR wrote in 2007 still stands today: Control in Afghanistan essentially depends on who is standing where at any given time. The situation remains extremely fluid, largely because of mobility advantages on both sides. Taliban forces have mobility advantages over foreign forces due their self-sufficiency. Taliban conscripts do not rely on lengthy, tenuous supply chains that cross over politically and militarily hostile territory. They are local fighters who depend on family and friends for supplies and shelter or, when forced, use intimidation to take what they need from civilians. They can also easily blend into their surroundings. These abilities translate into superior tactical mobility.

An example of the control that the Taliban have on the ground is opium production. In poppy-producing areas of the south and west, locals rely on the Taliban for protecting, purchasing and moving their product to market. In these areas, the Taliban have not only physical leverage over civilians but also economic leverage, which helps strengthen allegiances. While opium production in Helmand, the province with the highest rate of poppy cultivation, dropped by one-third over the past year, poppy production continues to increase in other provinces such as Kandahar, Farah and especially Badghis, where poppy production increased 93 percent (along with attacks) over the past year. This province — and the north/northwest of

Afghanistan in general — is an area that certainly bears watching since it has traditionally not been a Taliban stronghold.

Bound by supply-chain limitations, foreign forces and the Afghan forces modeled after them can be less flexible and spontaneous than the strategy might dictate, resulting in predictable troop movements and a reliance on stationary bases, which can be easily targeted by the Taliban.

However, what U.S. and ISAF forces have that the Taliban do not is air superiority. Foreign forces have been able to deny the Taliban sanctuaries by using air surveillance and air strikes that can neutralize large contingents of Taliban fighters and commanders without putting U.S. and ISAF forces in harm's way. Air superiority gives foreign forces an advantage over the Taliban's superior ground mobility and denies the Taliban complete control over any territory. However, air superiority does not guarantee control over any specific territory, since ground control is required to administer territory through organized government. This arrangement creates concentric circles of influence. The Taliban may patrol one stretch of land one day and U.S. forces may patrol the same stretch of ground the next. Similarly, village allegiances shift constantly to avoid being perceived by foreign forces as harboring Taliban, lest the village become the target of an airstrike. At the same time, the village must maintain cordial relations with the local Taliban to avoid harsh reprisals.

Additionally, foreign forces are able to use air power to overcome some of their supply-chain limitations and vulnerabilities by relying on helicopter transport for shuttling supplies and deploying troops. Helicopters greatly reduce reliance on ground transport but they are in short supply and, in an environment where counter-tactics develop as quickly as tactics, they have their own vulnerabilities.

Remaining Realities

Just as foreign and Afghan forces struggle to control of territory, so do the Taliban. Even during the days of the Islamic Emirate, when the Taliban were at their peak, considerable swaths of territory in the north eluded their control. The fact remains that Afghanistan's geography and ethnic/tribal makeup ensure that any power seeking to control Afghanistan will face a serious struggle. With flat, unprotected borderlands where most of its people live and a mountainous center, Afghanistan is both highly susceptible to foreign interference and governed poorly from any centralized location. While many of its neighbors can easily project power into it, they are unable or unwilling to rule it outright.

The Taliban Strategy
Feb. 24, 2010

The Taliban were never defeated in 2001, when the United States moved to topple their government in the wake of the 9/11 attacks. As STRATFOR pointed out at the time, they largely declined combat in the face of overwhelmingly superior military force. Though they were not, at that moment, an insurgent force, their moves were classic guerrilla behavior, and their quick transition from the seat of power back to such tactics is a reminder of how well — and how painfully — schooled Afghans have been in the insurgent arts over the last several decades.

While the U.S.-led coalition never stopped pursuing the Taliban, Washington's attention quickly shifted to Iraq. In Afghanistan, the mission quickly evolved from toppling a government in Kabul to combating a nascent insurgency in the south and east. U.S. officials, led by the American ambassador to Kabul, Zalmay Khalilzad, first began the process of talking to the Taliban on the eve of the invasion of Iraq. All this took place while Washington continued to press Islamabad to do more against the Taliban.

And though it took the Taliban a while to regroup, a considerable vacuum began to grow in which the Taliban began to re-emerge, particularly amid poor, corrupt and ineffectual central governance. As early as 2006, it was clear that the Afghan jihadist movement had assumed the form of a growing and powerful insurgency that was progressively gaining steam; the situation was beginning to approach the point at which it could no longer be ignored. As the surge in Iraq began to show signs of success, the United States began to shift its attention back to Afghanistan.

It was thus clear to the Taliban long before U.S. President Barack Obama's long-anticipated announcement that some 30,000 additional troops would be sent to Afghanistan in 2010 that there would be more of a fight before the United States and its allies would be willing to abandon the country — a surge that is an attempt, in part, to reshape Taliban perceptions of the timeline of the conflict by redoubling the American commitment before the drawdown might begin.

Overall, the Taliban ideally aspire to return to the height of their power in the late 1990s but realize that this is not realistic. That ascent to power, which followed the toppling of the Marxist regime left in place after the Soviet withdrawal and the 1992-1996 intra-Islamist civil war, was somewhat anomalous in that the circumstances were fairly unique to post-Soviet invasion Afghanistan. Today, the Taliban's opponents are much stronger and far better equipped to challenge the Taliban than in the mid-1990s; this opposing force is as much a reality as the Taliban and has a vested interest in preserving the current regime. The old mujahideen of the 1980s, whom the younger Taliban displaced in the 1990s, have grown steadily wealthier since the collapse of the Taliban regime and are now well-settled and prosperous in Kabul and their respective regions, benefiting greatly from the Western presence and Western money. This is true of many urban areas of Afghanistan that have been altered significantly in the eight years since the U.S. invasion and have little desire to return the Taliban's severe austerity. In many ways, this fight for dominance is between not only the Taliban and the United States and its allies; it is also between the Taliban and the old Islamist elite, the former mujahideen leaders who did their time on the battlefield in the 1980s.

So, in addition to fighting the current military battle, there is a great deal of factional fighting and political maneuvering with other Afghan centers of power. At a bare minimum, the Taliban intend to ensure that they remain the single strongest power in the country, with not only the largest share of the pie in Kabul (the ability to dominate) but also a significant degree of power and autonomy within their core areas in the south and east of the country. But within the movement (which is a very diffuse and complex set of entities) there is a great deal of debate about what objectives are reasonably achievable. Like the Shia in Iraq, who originally aspired to total dominance in the early days following the fall of the Baathist regime and have since moderated their goals, the Taliban have recognized that some degree of power sharing is necessary. The ultimate objective of the Taliban — resumption of power at the national level — is somewhat dependent on how events play out in the coming years. The objective of attaining the apex of power is not in dispute, but the best avenue — be it reconciliation or fighting it out until the United States begins to draw down — and how exactly that apex might be defined is still being debated.

But there is an important caveat to the Taliban's ambitions. Having held power in Kabul, they are wary of returning there in a way that would ultimately render them an international pariah state, as they were in the 1990s. When the Taliban first came to power, only Pakistan, Saudi Arabia and the United Arab Emirates recognized the regime, and the group's leadership became intimately familiar with the challenges of attempting to govern a country without wider international recognition. It was under this isolation that the Taliban allied with al Qaeda, which provided them with men, money and equipment. Now it is using al Qaeda again, this time not just as a force multiplier but, even more important, as a potential bargaining chip at the negotiating table. Mullah Omar, the Taliban's central leader, wants to get off the international terrorist watch list, and there have been signals from various elements of the Taliban that the group is willing to abandon al Qaeda for the right price. This countervailing consideration also contributes to the Taliban's objective — and particularly the means to achieving that objective — remaining in flux.

To understand the Taliban and their current strategy, it helps to begin with the basics. The Taliban are insurgents, and their first order of business is simply survival. A domestic guerrilla group almost always has more staying power than an occupier, which is projecting force over a greater distance and has the added burden of a domestic population less directly committed to a war in a foreign — and often far-off — land. If the Taliban can only survive as a cohesive and coherent entity until the United States and its allies leave Afghanistan, they will have a far less militarily capable opponent (Kabul) with whom to compete for dominance.

Currently facing an opponent (the United States) that has already stipulated a timetable for withdrawal, the Taliban are in an enviable position. The United States has given itself an extremely aggressive and ambitious set of goals to be achieved in a very short period of time. If the Taliban can both survive and disrupt American efforts to lay the foundations for a U.S./NATO withdrawal, their prospects for ultimately achieving their aims increase dramatically.

And here the strategy to achieve their imperfectly defined objective begins to take shape. The Taliban have no intention of completely evaporating into the countryside, and they have every intention of continuing to harass International Security Assistance Force (ISAF) troops, inflicting casualties and raising the cost of continued occupation. In so doing, the Taliban not only retain their relevance but may also be able to hasten the withdrawal of foreign forces.

Judging from the initial phase of Operation Moshtarak in Marjah and what can likely be expected in similar offensives in other areas, the Taliban strategy toward the surge is: 1) largely decline combat but leave behind a force significant enough to render the securing phase as difficult as is possible for U.S.-led coalition forces by using hit-and-run tactics and planting improvised explosive devices; 2) once the coalition force becomes overwhelming, fall back and allow the coalition to set up shop and wage guerrilla and suicide attacks (though Mullah Omar has issued guidance that these attacks should be initiated only after approval at the highest levels in order to minimize civilian casualties). In all likelihood, this phase of the Taliban campaign would include attempts at intimidation and subversion against Afghan security forces.

Being a diffuse guerrilla movement, the Taliban will likely attempt to replicate this strategy as broadly as possible, forcing ISAF forces to expend more energy than they would prefer on holding ground while impeding the building and reconstruction phase, which will become increasingly difficult as coalition forces target more and more areas. The idea is that the locals who are already wary about relying on Kabul and its Western allies will then become even more disenchanted with the ability of the coalition to weaken the Taliban. However, the ISAF attempting to take control of key bases of support on which the Taliban have long relied, and the impact of these efforts on the Taliban, will warrant considerable scrutiny.

For now, the Taliban appear to have lost interest in larger-scale attacks involving several hundred fighters being committed to a single objective. Though such attacks certainly garner headlines, they are extremely costly in terms of manpower and materiel with little practical gain. And with old strongholds like Helmand province feeling the squeeze, there are certainly some indications that ISAF offensives are taking an appreciable bite out of the operational capabilities of at least the local Taliban commanders.

Conserving forces and minimizing risk to their core operational capability are parallel and interrelated considerations for the Taliban in terms of survival. If the recent assault on Marjah is any indication, the Taliban are adhering to these principles. While some fighters did dig in and fight and while resistance has stiffened — especially within the last week — the Taliban declined to make it a bloody compound-to-compound fight despite the favorable defensive terrain.

Similarly, the U.S. surge intends to make it hard for the Taliban to sustain — much less replace — manpower and materiel. Taliban tactics must be tailored to maximize damage to the enemy while minimizing costs, which drives the Taliban directly to hit-and-run tactics and the widespread use of improvised explosive devices.

There is little doubt that the Taliban will continue to inflict casualties in the coming year. But there is also considerable resolve behind the surge, which will not even be up to full strength until the summer and will be maintained until at least July 2011. Indeed, it is not clear if the Taliban can inflict enough casualties to alter the American timetable in its favor any further.

There is also the underlying issue of sustaining the resistance. Manpower and logistics are inescapable parts of warfare. Though the United States and its allies bear the heavier burden, the Taliban cannot ignore that they are losing key population centers and opium-growing areas central to recruitment, financing and sanctuary. The parallel crackdowns by the ISAF on the Afghan side of the border and the Pakistani crackdowns on the opposite side, where the Taliban has long enjoyed sanctuary, represent a significant challenge to the Taliban if the efforts can be sustained. Signs of a potential increase in cooperation and coordination between Washington and Islamabad could also be significant.

In other words, despite all its flaws, there is a coherency to what the United States is attempting to achieve. Success is anything but certain, but the United States does seek to make very real inroads against the core strength of the Taliban. One of those methods is to reduce the Taliban's operational capability to the point where it will no longer have the capability to overwhelm Afghan security forces after the United States begins to draw down. There is no shortage of issues surrounding the U.S. objectives to train up the Afghan National Army and National Police, and it is not at all clear that even if those objectives are met that indigenous forces will be able to manage the Taliban.

But the Taliban must also deal with the logistical strain being imposed on them and strive to maintain their numbers and indigenous support. Central to this effort is the Taliban's information operations (IO), conveying their message to the Afghan people. Thus far, the ISAF has been far behind the Taliban in such IO efforts, but as the coalition ratchets up the pressure, it remains to be seen whether the more abstract IO will be sufficient for sustaining hard logistical support, especially with pressure being applied on both sides of the border.

Similarly, there is the issue of internal coherency. Any insurgent movement must deal with not only the occupier but also other competing guerrillas and insurgents, whether their central focus is military power or ideological power. The Taliban's main competition is entrenched in the regime of President Hamid Karzai and among those in opposition to Karzai but part of the state; at issue are the Taliban's sometimes loose affiliations with other Taliban elements and al Qaeda. The United States, the Karzai regime, Pakistan and al Qaeda are all seeking and applying leverage anywhere they can to hive off reconcilable elements of the Taliban.

The United States seeks to divide the pragmatic elements of the Taliban from the more ideological ones. The Karzai regime may be willing to deal with them in a more coherent fashion, but at the heart of all its considerations is the partially incompatible retention of its own power. Al Qaeda, with its own survival on the line, is seeking to draw the Taliban toward its transnational agenda. Meanwhile, Pakistan wants to bring the Taliban to heel, primarily so it can own the negotiating process and consolidate its position as the dominant power in Afghanistan, much as Iran seeks to do in Iraq. Each player has different motivations, objectives and timetables.

Amidst all these tensions, the Taliban must expend intelligence efforts and resources to maintain cohesion, despite being an inherently local and decentralized phenomenon. As Mullah Omar's code of conduct released in July 2009 demonstrates, "command" of the Taliban as an insurgent group is not as firm as it is in more rigid organizational hierarchies. The reconciliation efforts will certainly test the Taliban's coherency.

If history is any judge, in the long run the Taliban will retain the upper hand. In Afghanistan, the United States is attempting to do something that has never been tried before — much less achieved — i.e., constitute a viable central government from scratch in the midst of a guerrilla war. But the Taliban must be concerned about the possibility that some aspects of the U.S. strategy may succeed. Central to the American effort will be Pakistan — and Islamabad is showing significant signs of wanting to work closer with Washington.

Peace Talks and Hizb-i-Islami's Aims
March 22, 2010

Afghan President Hamid Karzai has met with a delegation from militant group Hizb-i-Islami for peace talks, a government spokesman said March 22. The delegation is reportedly led by former Afghan Prime Minister Qutbuddin Helal, deputy to Hizb-i-Islami leader and renowned Afghan warlord Gulbuddin Hekmatyar, and the meeting comes on the heels of clashes between Hizb-i-Islami and Taliban fighters in Baghlan province.

While Hizb-i-Islami is the second-largest Pashtun Islamist militant faction in Afghanistan after the Taliban, it is also a much smaller group. If it does reach an accommodation with the government, the defection would be an important political coup for the Karzai government but would not necessarily signal a readiness by the wider Taliban movement to negotiate.

Hekmatyar has a reputation for being quick to change sides for personal gain and, like many militant leaders, is alleged to have killed a large number of civilians and committed atrocities against women during the 1992-1996 intra-Islamist civil war. Hekmatyar also remains close to the Pakistanis, a relationship that reaches back to the 1970s. During the Soviet war, the Pakistani government under Gen. Mohammed Zia-ul-Haq shared a similar Islamist outlook with Hekmatyar's Hizb-i-Islami, and Pakistani support made Hekmatyar Islamabad's strongest ally among Afghanistan's insurgents at the time. Over the years, the relationship has taken many forms, but Hekmatyar has remained an important Pakistani asset in Afghanistan, even as he has grown closer to Iran (where he lived in exile for many years). These ties to Tehran, as well as al Qaeda and the Taliban, make Hekmatyar a concern for Washington; he would also be likely to figure into any U.S.-Iranian dealings on Afghanistan.

Both Kabul and Islamabad are attempting control the negotiations with Hekmatyar, just as both are attempting to control the wider negotiation and political settlement process in order to safeguard their own interests in shaping the political landscape in the lead-up to an eventual U.S. and NATO withdrawal. But the interests of the United States — and to a lesser extent Iran — must also be factored into any political accommodation.

The opening negotiating position that the Hizb-i-Islami delegation has brought to Kabul — reportedly the withdrawal of all U.S. and foreign military forces within six months and the ultimate dissolution of the Karzai government — is obviously not going to happen. But merely by traveling to Kabul and meeting with Karzai, the group has separated itself from the most intransigent of Afghanistan's militant actors and may well be willing to further moderate its position.

The initial terms offered by Hekmatyar would attempt to carve out a position for himself separate from the Taliban in the hope that many fighters will join him, especially in the east (where the Taliban and Hizb-i-Islami are in more direct conflict) and north (which is less strongly Pashtun and where the Taliban has only recently begun to stage a comeback).

The Taliban are watching Hekmatyar's moves and understand that they must maintain cohesion among their disparate elements. The recent fighting in Baghlan province may be a sign of things to come for Hekmatyar's fighters and civilian loyalists as the Taliban attempt to ensure that their own myriad factions do not begin to be hived off and pulled into Kabul's camp.

Like the Taliban, Hizb-i-Islami is itself a movement riddled with personal and ideological fissures, and while it may offer some wider grounds for reconciliation between the Afghan government and the country's militant actors, it is highly unlikely to make much headway in supplanting the Taliban. So while Karzai has much to gain from playing up the negotiations, the Hizb-i-Islami effort — while not necessarily insignificant — is not "dividing" the Taliban and is insufficient on its own to achieve the sort of broad political accommodation that the American strategy requires.

Afghanistan as a Hub of the Global Trade in Illicit Opiates
March 29, 2010

At a NATO conference in Brussels March 24, NATO spokesman James Appathurai rejected suggestions from Russian counternarcotics director Viktor Ivanov that an opium crop eradication program be implemented in Afghanistan. Over the past 20 years, Russia has gone from being a trans-shipment route for heroin to being a major consumer of heroin, the second largest market in the world behind Europe. Such a development has dramatic effects on public health and social stability in a country already facing dire demographic challenges, so it makes sense that Russia would take an interest in eliminating the source of the drugs.

However, opium cultivation has become a main source of income for thousands of rural Afghans, and as we recently saw in the NATO-led push into southern Afghanistan's Helmand province, making peace with the locals by not interfering with their livelihood is a higher priority than eradicating their opium poppies. Right now, as a new counterinsurgency strategy takes shape in Afghanistan, Russian counternarcotics officials are unlikely to get much cooperation from NATO when it comes to the destruction of crops. That will likely come in time. The Russians may find more immediate cooperation in interdicting opiate trafficking in Afghanistan, which is largely managed by militant factions opposing NATO forces.

Afghanistan is at the center of the global trade in illicit opiates, with more than 90 percent of the world's opium supply originating there. (The country also is a huge cultivator of marijuana, which is a significant cash crop but not as significant as opium.) Despite the fact control routes to and profits from the primary consumer markets in Iran, Russia and Europe.

Production

Opiates are the family of refined narcotics to which heroin, morphine, codeine and other often-abused substances belong. Opiates such as morphine were developed in the 19th century for medicinal purposes and are still widely used (although much more restricted) today. Heroin is processed in a way that allows faster absorption into the system, making it a more potent form of morphine. Both, along with other related drugs, are refined from opium, a naturally occurring product of the opium poppy plant.

Opium is produced by slitting the seed pod of opium poppies to extract the sap. The sap oozes out as a thick brown-black gum that is then formed into bricks that are sold to traffickers and distributors. The poppy growing season in Afghanistan runs from planting in December to harvest in April. But the growing season does not greatly affect the times of the year that the drugs are trafficked, since Afghan farmers and traffickers have built up an opium stockpile of approximately 12,000 tons, which is enough to supply about two years worth of global demand. Only 10 percent of this stockpile is in the hands of Afghan farmers, with the rest under the control of traffickers and militants both in Afghanistan and along the trafficking routes. This stockpile buffers against extreme market fluctuations by providing a steady stream of product that evens out the spike in supply during harvesting season, and it also serves as a safety net in case of seizures or crop destruction. This suggests a fairly high level of planning and organization among those trafficking opiates.

After the opium is collected by farmers it is usually sold to traffickers, who will often refine the opium further before moving it out of Afghanistan. In Afghanistan, this system is well organized, with farmers and traffickers often having agreements that run for several years. About 60 percent of the opium produced in Afghanistan is processed into heroin and, to a lesser extent, morphine, before being

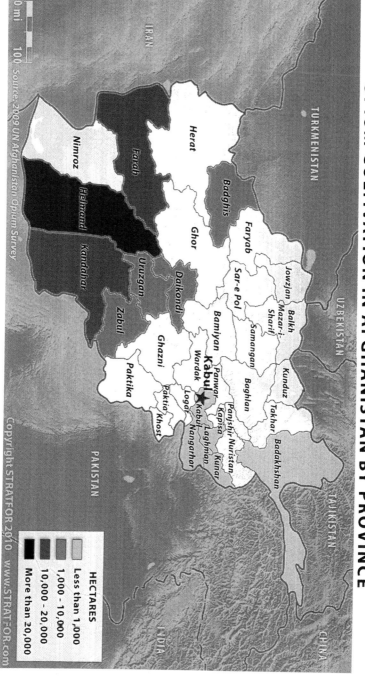

OPIUM CULTIVATION IN AFGHANISTAN BY PROVINCE

0 mi

100

Source: 2009 UN Afghanistan Opium Survey

Copyright STRATFOR 2010   www.STRATFOR.com

HECTARES

Less than 1,000
1,000 - 10,000
10,000 - 20,000
More than 20,000

TURKMENISTAN

UZBEKISTAN

TAJIKISTAN

CHINA

IRAN

PAKISTAN

INDIA

Herat
Farah
Nimroz
Badghis
Ghor
Helmand
Kandahar
Uruzgan
Daikondi
Zabul
Faryab
Sar-e Pol
Jowzjan
Mazar-i-Sharif
Balkh
Samangan
Bamiyan
Ghazni
Paktika
Wardak
Kabul
Panjwai
Baghlan
Kunduz
Takhar
Kapisa
Panjshir Nuristan
Badakhshan
Logar
Paktia
Khost
Kabul
Laghman
Kunar
Nangarhar

that opium poppies can be grown in a variety of climates and soil conditions, its production is so concentrated in Afghanistan and countries like it because the cultivation of opium poppies can thrive only in regions with limited government control. Within Afghanistan, the cultivation of poppies is concentrated in the south and west of the country, with Helmand province alone accounting for more than half of Afghanistan's total production. These are also the regions of the country where Afghan government control is the weakest and Taliban control is the strongest.

Besides Afghanistan, the other big opium producers are Myanmar, Pakistan, Laos and Mexico, but these countries make up only a fraction of overall production. Southeast Asia previously dominated opium production during the 1970s and most of the 1980s, while Afghanistan's opium was consumed regionally. It was not until the mid-1990s that Afghanistan went from being one of several large opium-growing countries to producing more than 50 percent of the world's supply. As Afghanistan's importance in the global opiate trade has grown, so has the value of trafficking routes out of the country. When Southeast Asian opium dominated the world market, Thailand and China were the main routes through which the product reached the consumer. Now, with Afghanistan producing most of the world's opium, Iran, Pakistan and Central Asia are the most important transit countries.

The trafficking of opiates out of Afghanistan to outside consumer markets is a highly lucrative business. The annual global market for illicit opiates is estimated to be about $65 billion, which, to put it in context, is roughly equal to the gross domestic product (GDP) of Croatia. In 2009, according to U.N. estimates, the opiate trade accounted for $2.3 billion of the Afghan economy, or about 19 percent of the country's GDP. The flow of drugs in one direction and money in the other is of strategic significance because it provides financial support for regional players, some of whom are militant groups like al Qaeda and the Taliban. Because production is centralized in Afghanistan, actors immediately surrounding Afghanistan

REGIONAL OPIATE TRAFFICKING ROUTES

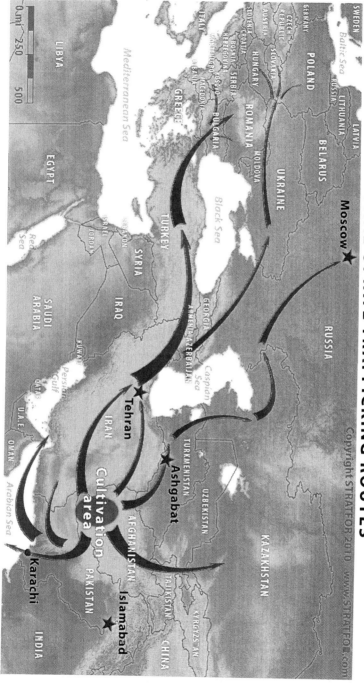

Copyright STRATFOR 2010 www.STRATFOR.com

moved out of the country. Refining also takes place all along the transit route from Afghanistan, especially in Iran and Russia, but it makes sense to refine the opium as close to the production site as possible. Refining opium into heroin and morphine gives traffickers a number of advantages over trafficking unrefined opium as a commodity. Heroin and morphine are more compact (10 kilograms of opium produce one kilogram of heroin), which makes it more efficient to transport. And one kilogram of heroin can fetch upwards of 100 times more than a kilogram of opium, making it more cost effective to transport.

The technology required to convert opium to heroin is very basic, requiring little more than a container to heat the opium in and some chemicals. However, some of the chemicals needed are difficult to acquire, acetic anhydride being the most important, and these have to be smuggled into Afghanistan. Anti-drug authorities have made a concerted effort to target the precursor trade, and this has made acquiring these chemicals in the necessary quantities (more than 13,000 tons a year) in Afghanistan difficult. However, refining in Afghanistan is still very common, and one sign of this has been the recent anthrax deaths of heroin users in Europe. The infected users were likely consuming heroin cut with ground-up goat bones, which is more prevalent in Afghanistan than the more commonly used sodium bicarbonate (baking soda) and is known to host anthrax spores.

Trafficking Routes

Illicit opiates are moved out of Afghanistan through three main routes. About 40 percent of Afghanistan's opiates travel through Iran to reach their end markets (which are mainly Russia, Europe and Iran), while 30 percent go through Pakistan and 25 percent go through central Asia, with the last 5 percent having an indeterminate route.

OPIATE TRAFFICKING BETWEEN AFGHANISTAN AND TURKMENISTAN

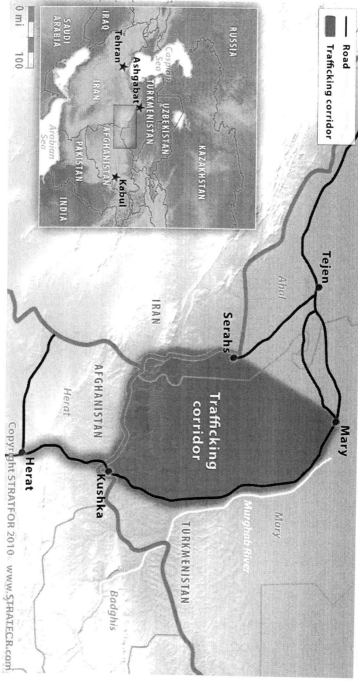

Road
Trafficking corridor

RUSSIA

Caspian Sea

Tehran
Ashgabat
TURKMENISTAN
UZBEKISTAN

IRAQ
SAUDI ARABIA
IRAN
KAZAKHSTAN

Arabian Sea
AFGHANISTAN
PAKISTAN
Kabul
INDIA

0 mi   100

Tejen

Ahal

Serahs

Mary

IRAN

Herat

AFGHANISTAN

Trafficking corridor

Kushka

Murghab River

Mary

TURKMENISTAN

Herat

Badghis

Copyright STRATFOR 2010   www.STRATFOR.com

Iran

Iran's land bridge connecting south Asia to the Middle East and Anatolian Peninsula has long been a trafficking route for all sorts of products, both licit and illicit. In 2007, more than 80 percent of the world's opium seizures and 28 percent of its heroin seizures were made in Iran. Since 1979 more than 3,600 police officers and soldiers have been killed in violence between the Iranian government and drug traffickers. Before Afghanistan became the world's leading opium-producing country, Iran was primarily a consumer of illicit opiates; trafficking through the country was very limited. This began to change as Afghanistan's importance in opium cultivation rose in the 1990s and Iran became the main route through which Afghan opiates reach the wealthy consumer markets in Europe (Iran is still a substantial consumer of opiates, particularly unrefined opium). Those opiates that are trafficked through Iran continue onward to Turkey and Azerbaijan, with the Turkish route being the most important, accounting for approximately 80 percent of the opiates consumed in Europe.

Afghan opiates enter Iran via three main routes: by land from Afghanistan, by land from Pakistan and by sea from Pakistan, with small amounts coming over the border to Turkmenistan. Within Iran the product is moved toward the northwestern regions of the country and on to Europe and Russia along two main routes. Drugs that come directly from Afghanistan are moved north of the Dasht-e-Kavir desert toward Tehran, and then on to Turkey or Azerbaijan. Most of what is smuggled in from Pakistan is moved south of the Kavir-e-Lut desert and then on toward Esfahan and Tehran. What is brought in by sea goes mainly to the ports of Bandar Abbas and Chabahar, before moving northwest with the rest of the flow. While opiates trafficked through Iran do go in other directions — mainly toward the Arabian Peninsula and into Iraq — most are bound for consumer markets in Europe or are consumed domestically. Once in Iran, the drugs are moved mainly by car and truck. Drug seizures are fairly common throughout Iran, but especially on the borders with

Afghanistan and Pakistan, along the northern and central corridors, and in Tehran.

Cross-border ethnic links are important to the smuggling of Afghan drugs in all of the countries of the region. This is particularly true in southeastern Iran, where the Baloch ethnic group is heavily involved in the drug trade. There are significant populations of Balochis in Iran, Afghanistan and Pakistan, and they move with relative ease between these countries. Government control over this border region is weak and traffickers move around in heavily armed groups with little fear of the authorities. Most of the drugs that cross the border in this region are transported by large, well-armed and motorized convoys. This is in contrast to the northern route, where drugs are more often brought over on foot or by camel or donkey — and frequently in the stomachs of these animals — before being loaded into vehicles for transit across Iran.

One reason that we know of Balochi involvement in drug trafficking between southwest Pakistan and Iran is that the Iranian government is anxious to associate militant separatist groups in the region with drug trafficking, and the Balochis in southern Iran are among the most active separatists in the country. News reports of raids and seizures along Iran's border with Pakistan tend to play up this aspect of the trade.

Little is known about the groups that are moving Afghan drugs through Iran, but given the substantial value of the drugs and the logistical management needed to ensure a steady flow of product, these groups seem to know what they are doing. The system must be organized at a higher level, and with the absence of official blame being placed on a nationwide organized-crime network, it is very likely that the Iranian government is involved. STRATFOR sources in Iran indicate that individual Islamic Revolutionary Guard Corps and military commanders oversee the flow of drugs through their regions, receiving a lucrative income in a country beset by multiple economic problems due to sanctions and the threat of more to come.

Given the value of opiates passing through Iran, estimated to be worth about $20 billion once they reach the street (approximately 5 percent of Iran's GDP), it is hard to believe that a state whose geography predisposes it to land trade would fight so hard to keep the financial boon linked to opiates out of the system. Seizures are still made across the country, but these are more likely triggered by traffickers who refuse to cooperate with the authorities managing the trade. In recent months Iranians have also been arrested for drug smuggling in a number of Southeast Asian countries, suggesting an expanded geographic scope for Iranian drug traffickers.

Pakistan

While Iran is the main trafficking route for Afghan-produced opiates, Pakistan is the most common first stop for drugs out of Afghanistan. The long border between the two countries is virtually impossible to control, and smuggling across the border is very common, especially for the Taliban. Indeed, opiate production and smuggling through Pakistan has provided essential support to the Afghan Taliban, which raised an estimated $450 million to $600 million between 2005 and 2008, according to the U.N. Office on Drugs and Crime.

Drugs enter the country along the northwest Afghan-Pakistani border and then take several paths across Pakistan. One is from southern Afghanistan across the border to the city of Quetta, which is an important transit point for Afghan opiates and a center of Afghan Taliban activity. About a quarter of the opiates that enter Pakistan are then taken into Iran through Balochistan province. Another important route is south through the Indus valley toward Karachi, a port city on the Arabian Sea and a key hub for organized crime in Pakistan. Once they leave the port of Karachi, the largest port in the region, drugs can be moved all over the world. Shipments of drugs are usually hidden in cargo containers, or they can be smuggled aboard commercial airliners. Afghan opiates moving through Pakistan also make their way to India and China, although Myanmar supplies most of the opiates to these markets.

Central Asia

Opiates moving north out of Afghanistan into Central Asia follow numerous routes. According to the United Nations, Tajikistan reported the most seizures in 2008, but tracking drug seizures does not necessarily indicate where most of the drugs are going. It does show where drug trafficking is the most volatile, where competing actors (including the government) are battling for turf and stealing each other's shipments. Afghan opiates are certainly trafficked north from Afghanistan through Uzbekistan, Tajikistan and Kyrgyzstan, but most of the northbound product goes through Turkmenistan along the northern route to Russia.

In many ways, this route is the most efficient one out of Afghanistan. Turkmenistan borders western Afghanistan, where some of the major opium-producing provinces are, so it is the shortest route north, linked to Afghanistan's northern trafficking route out of Herat. Also, the terrain between western Afghanistan and Turkmenistan, consisting for the most part of hilly desert that is very difficult to monitor, is relatively easy to traverse undetected. Uzbekistan's border with Afghanistan is relatively flat, but it is disconnected from Afghanistan's poppy-cultivating areas and defined in part by a river that is difficult to cross. Tajikistan also serves as a border crossing, since its western border with Afghanistan provides access (albeit through routes that are far from ideal) into Central Asia. Eastern Tajikistan, however, is covered in rugged mountains and very lightly populated, making the efficient trafficking of anything very difficult. Finally, traffickers in southern Turkmenistan have the benefit of working under the protection of the Mary clan, the largest of five major clans that dominate Turkmenistan's political landscape. Occupying Turkmenistan's Mary region, the clan is largely blocked from having any kind of real power in the government, but it has been given control of the lucrative drug trade in Turkmenistan in order to ensure its loyalty.

Crossing the border from Afghanistan to Turkmenistan is the trickiest part of the Central Asian journey. Avoiding government checkpoints is relatively easy, since the border is an uninhabited desert and traffickers can simply drive across in most places. However, they do face the threat of roaming bandits in search of profitable targets to rob — such as heroin smugglers. For this reason, traffickers are constantly changing their routes, taking advantage of a roughly 90-mile-wide and 130-mile-long desert corridor in southwestern Turkmenistan between the Iranian border and the Murghab River that is crisscrossed by a network of jeep paths created to evade bandits. Once traffickers get through this desert, they enter the protection of the Mary clan, which provides secure trafficking north to the Kazakh border.

From there, drugs pass through Kazakhstan and farther north to Russian consumer markets, hitting regional distribution hubs along the way to Moscow. Russian organized-crime groups (primarily the Moscow Mob) and elements within the Federal Security Service provide cover to traffickers along this route (for a price, of course).

Markets

The majority of Afghan opiates go to three main markets: Iran, Russia and Europe. Together they account for the consumption of about 66 percent of Afghan opiates. Iran is the main consumer of the unrefined opium, accounting for 42 percent of the world's total, while heroin is more common in Russia and Europe, accounting for 21 percent and 26 percent of the world's total, respectively. In the 1990s Russia was more of a transit market than a consumption market for opiates. This began to change in the late 1990s, when the rate of heroin use in Russia rose rapidly. Between 1998 and 1999, the number of Russian users increased 400 percent, absorbing much of the product that used to go on to other markets. As wealth in Russia (i.e., Moscow and St. Petersburg) rose over the past decade, the Russian consumer market helped absorb even more of the product flow. Recently, Afghan opiates also have begun to supply Chinese consumers and may now account for as much as 25 percent of that market. The United States, a huge market for illicit opiates, is low on the list because most of the heroin consumed there is produced in Colombia and Mexico.

Russia has largely become a consumer market for Afghan opiates, with southern land routes through Iran and Turkey and maritime routes taking over most of the supply to Europe. The significance of this is that countries along the southern trafficking routes, such as Pakistan, Iran and Turkey, are benefiting more from the financial gains of opiate trafficking while Russia is suffering more from the social strains of opiate use. Russia is estimated to have as many as 2.5 million consumers of illicit opiates, and the Russian government recently estimated that Russians spend $17 billion annually on Afghan opiates.

So it does make sense that post-Soviet Russia is starting to lobby for opium-crop eradication in Afghanistan. But it will not happen overnight. Winning hearts and minds is a painstaking process, and weaning farmers from a lucrative cash crop will take time. Popular support for the U.S./NATO mission has become a valuable currency in Afghanistan, as valuable as opium profits are to the growers and traffickers, and some kind of balance must be struck between the two. In the coming years, with the U.S. and NATO on watch, interdiction of traffickers may well take precedence over destroying the poppy fields of struggling Afghan farmers.

A Taliban Point of View
April 1, 2010

As any student of war knows, there are two sides to any conflict. The opposing side is not a passive entity to be acted upon but an active and creative enemy engaged in what Prussian theorist Carl von Clausewitz characterized as a "two-struggle." This is every bit as true in an insurgency, where the insurgent is waging an asymmetric struggle from a very different position and with very different strengths and weaknesses.

In all the strategic discussions about Gen. Stanley McChrystal's population-centric efforts in Afghanistan, combating the Taliban has been a comparatively rare point of discussion as rules of engagement are shifted to minimize collateral damage and civilian casualties, military offensives are announced publicly well in advance and emphasis is placed on establishing effective governance and civil authority. There is a clear rationale behind the thrust of American efforts to undermine the Taliban's base of support. But as recent developments in southern Afghanistan attest, the Taliban are not passively accepting those efforts.

At the same time, the Taliban are waging a classic guerrilla campaign — conducting hit-and-run attacks to wear down their adversary while avoiding decisive engagement. Their strategic incentive is to wait out the United States while conducting dispersed, economy-of-force efforts to prevent the U.S.-led International Security Assistance Force (ISAF) from achieving its goals within the aggressive and ambitious timetable to which Washington has committed itself.

So while the United States attempts to apply military force to lock down the security situation in key areas, its ultimate objective is much more difficult and seemingly tangential. The United States aims to achieve the positive objective of effecting meaningful shifts in perceptions and political circumstances that will undermine the Taliban's base of support while training and improving Afghan security forces. By comparison, the Taliban's negative objective of preventing American success is far simpler and more direct.

Thus, the Taliban's tactics and measures of success will be profoundly different than those of the United States. There is no doubt the Taliban's claims thus far have included an element of exaggeration, but their claims are critical to providing insight into the Taliban's information operations and how they perceive themselves and their efforts. For example, every day the Taliban make multiple claims about destroying numerous ISAF "tanks" across the country.

In truth, the number of main battle tanks in Afghanistan is rather limited, and the casualties inflicted are lower than the Taliban claim. Similarly, almost any armored vehicle in the country that the Taliban destroy or claim to destroy is reported as a "tank," so the word is best understood to signify anything from an actual main battle tank to a Stryker or even a mine-resistant, ambush-protected vehicle (both of which are wheeled).

But at the same time, both the Taliban and the ISAF are engaged in information operations (IO) and propaganda efforts designed to shape perceptions domestically and abroad. Although there are some urban exceptions, it is the Taliban that have established considerable IO dominance in Afghanistan. It is their message that is reaching the Afghan population in areas targeted by the ISAF to retake and deny the Taliban.

Similarly, even though a multiple-fatality improvised explosive device (IED) attack on an ISAF vehicle constitutes a bad day for the coalition, it is not seen as a strategic or operational-level event. But for the Taliban, it is precisely that. Just as the United States trumpets the capture of a midlevel Taliban commander or his death in an unmanned aerial vehicle strike, the Taliban consider inflicting pain on the "foreign occupier" with a successful IED strike a tactical and IO coup.

Of course, the loss of a midlevel Taliban commander may have more impact on the Taliban's operational capability than ISAF's loss of several front-line troops. But the IED has broader implications. If the vehicle belongs to a NATO ally with a particularly shaky commitment to the mission, or a particularly vocal opposition to the war at home, it can absolutely have a strategic impact if the death toll hastens that ally's withdrawal. But even in more normal, day-to-day scenarios, the IED can increase the threat level on that particular road. While few routes are "closed" this way, the convoy and force protection requirements can change, requiring additional commitments of vehicles and specialized units. This can make convoys more difficult to arrange and slow travel time as stops to investigate and disable IEDs become more frequent.

The IED continues to be the Taliban's single most effective tactic against the ISAF. While it is not yet clear whether Taliban IEDs have significantly impeded ISAF operations, their claims regarding IEDs serve to undermine U.S. attempts to shift perceptions held by ordinary Afghans. As long as the Taliban are widely perceived not only as resistance fighters — something akin to having a national identity in a country without one — but also as an undefeated and undefeatable reality, the incentive for Afghan locals is to limit their interaction with and support of local government and ISAF forces. This is because they fear being abandoned later, left to face the return of the Taliban to local power.

Like any entity, the Taliban also face the issue of credibility, which acts to limit the degree to which they can exaggerate claims about battlefield successes. But because they are so dominant in IO right now, it is not clear that these claims are perceived as being anything but reasonably close to the truth. So while it may be clear elsewhere that a given Taliban claim is exaggerated and inaccurate, that claim shapes perceptions where it matters — on the ground in Afghanistan — more than claims by the ISAF. Of course, since the United States also is engaged in IO and trying to shape domestic opinion, the ground truth generally lies somewhere in the middle.

Karzai as Political Reality
April 6, 2010

White House spokesman Robert Gibbs on Monday expressed fresh concerns over rare comments from Afghan President Hamid Karzai. The president criticized the United States and its Western allies for engaging in fraud in last year's presidential vote as part of efforts to deny him a second term. Gibbs told reporters, "The remarks are genuinely troubling. The substance of the remarks, as have been looked into by many, are obviously not true." Elsewhere, Karzai, in an interview with the BBC, stood behind accusations that the West was responsible for election fraud in Afghanistan, saying, "What I said about the election was all true, I won't repeat it, but it was all true."

Trading barbs with U.S. President Barack Obama's administration — twice in four days — is not the only thing Karzai has done. In a closed-door meeting with a select group of Afghan lawmakers, Karzai reportedly threatened to join the Taliban insurgency if he was continuously pressured by the West to engage in reforms. Lawmaker Farooq Marenai, who represents the northeastern province of Nangarhar, told AP that Karzai said that "if I come under foreign pressure, I might join the Taliban." Marenai added that Karzai remarked that the Taliban would then be redefined as a resistance movement fighting foreign occupation instead of being perceived as rebels trying to topple an elected government.

Karzai's spokesman has officially denied that the Afghan leader threatened to align with the jihadist movement. Whether or not Karzai made the statement is less important than the fact that relations between Karzai and Washington have seriously deteriorated. It is not clear that the United States has decided to withdraw its support from him, since Gibbs told reporters Monday that a May 12 meeting between Obama and Karzai at the White House was still being held as scheduled.

Despite the badly damaged relationship, Karzai cannot easily be replaced. He became president as part of a compromise after the fall of the Taliban regime because Taliban fighters assassinated Abdul Haq — Washington's first choice — in October 2001. Since then he has managed all the various regional warlords and factions (save the Taliban, of course) in an effort to hold the country together.

That the Karzai regime is corrupt is nothing new. It has been for the past eight years. But the United States has never been interested in getting rid of Karzai for the simple fact that a replacement would be hard to find. During his tenure, Karzai has been built up so much that even good possible replacements do not exist, at least ones capable of dealing effectively with the Taliban.

At this point it is not clear that Washington wants or is able to get rid of the only leader Afghanistan has known in the post-Taliban period. Karzai also has strong incentives to appear tough in public and distance himself from the Americans — especially to dispel accusations that he is merely a puppet. Some of this could well be manufactured as Karzai attempts to consolidate power following contentious elections.

The important question is: How deep do these tensions run? There is no shortage of Karzai critics in Washington, so it is important to realize that the extent to which the tensions are real is symptomatic of deeper functional rifts. Karzai is as much a political reality in Afghanistan as the Taliban, and he has only just now begun a second five-year term. Rifts aside, Karzai is an inescapable player in this extremely pivotal year in Afghanistan.

The View from Kabul
April 20, 2010

A growing Taliban insurgency and a surge of U.S. and allied forces into the country are shaking things up in Kabul, Afghanistan's capital. There, Afghan President Hamid Karzai, now in his second five-year term, has been formally in power since 2002 and in elected office since 2004. After several years of being portrayed as an American lackey, perceived more as the mayor of Kabul than the president of Afghanistan, Karzai has tried to break out of this mold and secure his own political survival. This at a time when the Taliban have emerged as a major force and the United States has made it clear that its commitment to Afghanistan is limited.

Karzai's problems have only escalated since the Obama administration took office. Relations began to sour in the run-up to last year's Afghan presidential election, when elements in Washington began searching for alternatives to Karzai, who was being criticized for corruption. But with years of experience in managing his country's many regional warlords, Karzai was able to quickly align with all major ethnic groups and ensure his victory in the election, despite the entire process being marred by charges of fraud.

Tensions with Washington throughout the election helped Karzai create his own political space within the country, space that he sought to expand even as U.S. Ambassador to Afghanistan Karl Eikenberry expressed doubts behind the scenes about Karzai's viability as an effective American partner. In recent weeks, Karzai took his efforts to a different level by accusing the United States of engaging in fraud during the Afghan election, triggering a strong response from Washington. His move paid off. After a couple of weeks of high tensions, senior U.S. officials, including President Barack Obama, moved to ease the strain, calling the Afghan president an ally and partner. With almost all of a second five-year term still ahead of him, Karzai is as much a political reality in the country as the Taliban.

Objectives and Problems

The main objective of the current Karzai regime is to maintain as much of the existing political structure as possible and maximize its position within that structure. This is a system that has been crafted and staffed in large part by Karzai and his inner circle, and thus it bolsters their position disproportionately. But because the Taliban are also a political reality, Kabul must work to achieve meaningful political accommodations that will serve to stabilize the security situation in the countryside.

To maximize its leverage, Kabul must do this rapidly. The surge of U.S. forces into the country and the money, aid and advice that the Karzai regime receives will never be more abundant than it is right now, so with his power at its height, Karzai must reach these political accommodations as soon as possible.

Meanwhile, Kabul has two main problems. The first is that it has limited means to compel the Taliban to negotiate on the requisite timetable while the Taliban have every incentive to hold out on any meaningful talks. The Karzai government is working with interlocutors (mostly former Taliban officials who still retain influence) to negotiate with the jihadist movement, but the question is the pace at which real progress can be made. At the heart of these negotiations is the question of who speaks for the Pashtuns, Afghanistan's single largest demographic segment, accounting for more than 40 percent of the country's population.

Nor will political accommodation come cheaply. The Taliban will not be won over with a few Cabinet positions. The current discussions include the need for constitutional change that will allow more room for Islamic law and perhaps an extra-executive religious entity that controls the judiciary. Just how much of a stake the Taliban would have in the government and what shape that stake would take remains to be seen. In any case, it will likely require substantial concessions in Kabul.

The second problem is that Kabul's efforts to negotiate with the Taliban are being pulled and manipulated from all sides. This is the real challenge for the current regime — balancing all the outside players who are trying to shape the negotiations. Kabul needs to prevent the already fractious and war-torn country from becoming a proxy battleground for the United States and Iran or Pakistan and India (among other countries). The difficulty of maintaining this balancing act — while also maintaining local support — is increasing by the day.

Kabul's closest allies are the United States and the NATO-led International Security Assistance Force (ISAF). Although Washington and Kabul do not always see eye to eye, and Karzai is trying to distance himself from the United States in order to downplay the puppet image, the United States and other coalition countries provide the foundational support for his government as well as security in the countryside. And while the United States likely views Karzai as a convenient scapegoat as well as an interchangeable political part, it is trying to demonstrate some confidence in the Afghan president. At a major tribal meeting in Kandahar on April 4,

U.S. Gen. Stanley McChrystal, head of the ISAF, was notably silent, allowing Karzai to speak and lead the discussion.

Aside from the United States, Pakistan is the next biggest player in Afghanistan, and because of its own links to the Taliban, it has far more practical leverage than the United States does in shaping the negotiations (of which it has every intention of being at the center). Pakistan's arrest of senior Taliban figure Mullah Abdul Ghani Baradar is now believed to have been carried out to disrupt direct negotiations between the Taliban and Kabul in which Baradar is thought to have been engaged. A strong Pakistani hand in Afghanistan is a longstanding reality for Kabul, but Islamabad is maneuvering to consolidate its influence as a planned American drawdown in 2011 approaches.

But Pakistan's resurging role in Afghanistan places Karzai in a difficult place between his eastern neighbor and its regional rival India. New Delhi has invested a great deal in development and reconstruction work in Afghanistan since 2002, and Kabul will need to balance this aid with the need for Pakistani assistance with the Taliban. Complicating all this, of course, is India's alignment with Russia on the Afghanistan issue.

Perhaps more critical than the Indo-Pakistani struggle over Afghanistan is the U.S.-Iranian contest. Although Iraq is the main arena for Washington's struggle with Tehran, the focus of the contest is shifting to Afghanistan, along with the U.S. military effort. Iran also has considerable influence to its east, with deep historical, ethno-linguistic and cultural ties that it has adroitly established and cultivated not only among its natural allies — ethno-political minorities opposed to the Taliban — but also among some elements of the Taliban themselves. Though this influence is not decisive (the Taliban have their own interests, and many groups opposed to the Taliban are close to Karzai and the West), Tehran has the ability to influence events on the ground in Afghanistan, and an eventual settlement of the war cannot happen without Iranian involvement. From Karzai's point of view, he has to balance his alignment with the United States with the fact that Iran is always going to be Afghanistan's western neighbor, long after U.S. and NATO forces have left his country.

This is really the ultimate problem. On its best day, Afghanistan is poor, lacks basic infrastructure and is economically hobbled. With weak domestic security forces and little to offer the outside world, Kabul can only hope to continue to entice more international aid while playing all the various countries with vested interests in Afghanistan against each other. Incorporating the Taliban into the political framework will be especially important over the next few years, but when and if that happens, the balancing act will continue to be played by any central government in Kabul.

CHAPTER 3: THE BORDER

Between Afghanistan and Pakistan: The Battlespace
Oct. 14, 2008

U.S. military cross-border operations from Afghanistan into Pakistan have become increasingly overt and unilateral since the spring. More than a tactical shift, these operations are meant to address the strategic problem of Pakistan's lawless Federally Administered Tribal Areas (FATA), where Taliban fighters from Afghanistan rest, recuperate and resupply and where other jihadists mount a growing Islamist insurgency in Pakistan. The next U.S. president will soon be working closely with the new head of U.S. Central Command, Gen. David Petraeus, on developing and implementing a new strategy for Afghanistan. This strategy will have to address the situation in Pakistan, where FATA sanctuaries for al Qaeda and Taliban fighters are reminiscent of North Vietnamese army sanctuaries in Laos and Cambodia during the Vietnam War.

Terrain

The northern part of the Afghan-Pakistani border is delineated by the Hindu Kush, a western subrange of the Himalayas that is at its highest elevations in the north, where a long and narrow spit of Afghan territory runs all the way to the Chinese border. The Hindu

Kush rises above the disputed territory of Kashmir and feeds into the Himalayas, which are the world's tallest mountains. Harsh, rugged terrain that is sparsely populated, the Hindu Kush is all but impassible and therefore useless for logistical purposes.

South of the Hindu Kush, the Afghan-Pakistani border begins to follow a ridgeline that drops precipitously to the Khyber Pass. Because Afghanistan is completely unconnected to the rail networks of its neighbors, the road from Peshawar, Pakistan, through the Khyber Pass and on to Jalalabad (and from there to Kabul) is a crucial lifeline for Afghanistan. The border rises up another ridge south of the Khyber and follows a mountain range known as the Safed Koh, which runs north-south, more or less the orientation of the border for several hundred miles. Though still mountainous, this area is rife with passes and trails used for infiltration in both directions — and particularly for moving supplies and fighters west into Afghanistan.

Below South Waziristan, the southernmost agency of the FATA, the border cuts westerly over the Toba Kakar range toward the second vital road link across the border, running from Quetta in western Pakistan to Kandahar in southeastern Afghanistan. Known as Balochistan province's Pashtun corridor (named for the dominant ethno-linguistic group in eastern and southern Afghanistan and in Pakistan's FATA, North-West Frontier Province [NWFP] and Balochistan province), this sector of the border encompasses an area where STRATFOR believes Taliban chief Mullah Omar is hiding. The border then follows the vast openness of Afghanistan's Kandahar province, where the terrain is less difficult to traverse but also offers far less concealment from the prying eyes of unmanned aerial vehicles (UAVs). This region is also sparsely populated with little in the way of infrastructure to facilitate the movement of military supplies.

This geography is a fixed reality for border operations. There are passes that are suitable for transit by pack animal or even motorbikes and four-wheel-drive vehicles and there are passes that can only be traveled by people on foot and in single file. It is not that insurgents create a new infiltration point when one is shut down by U.S. or NATO security operations but that there are so many potential

PAKISTAN'S FRONTIER

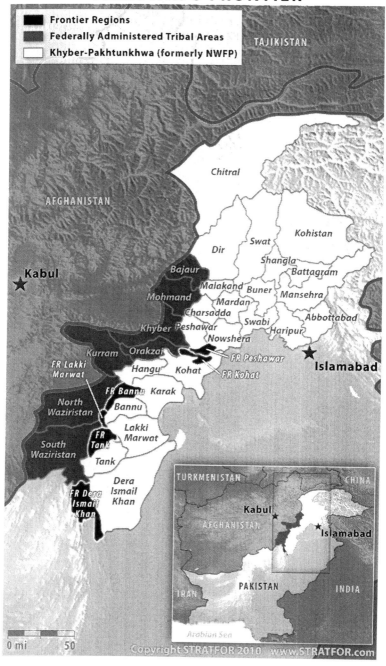

Legend:
- Frontier Regions
- Federally Administered Tribal Areas
- Khyber-Pakhtunkhwa (formerly NWFP)

TAJIKISTAN

Chitral

AFGHANISTAN

Kabul

Dir
Swat
Kohistan
Shangla
Battagram
Bajaur
Malakand
Buner
Mansehra
Mohmand
Mardan
Charsadda
Abbottabad
Khyber Peshawar
Swabi
Nowshera
Haripur
FR Peshawar
Orakzai
Kurram
FR Kohat
Islamabad
FR Lakki Marwat
Hangu
Kohat
FR Bannu
Karak
North Waziristan
Bannu
Lakki Marwat
FR Tank
South Waziristan
Tank
FR Dera Ismail Khan
Dera Ismail Khan

TURKMENISTAN
CHINA
Kabul
Islamabad
AFGHANISTAN
IRAN
PAKISTAN
INDIA
Arabian Sea

0 mi   50

Copyright STRATFOR 2010   www.STRATFOR.com

infiltration points in key sectors that infiltrators can vary locations of ingress and egress and have a good chance of success. Western troops, burdened by a multitude of security missions inside Afghanistan proper, are too limited in number to cover all of these points.

Another fixed reality is weather. Combat operations in the Afghan-Pakistani border area take on a regular cycle in accordance with the seasons. Winter arrives early in the extremely high altitudes of the Hindu Kush and Safed Koh. When the snows come, many of the high mountain passes become impassable, causing a noticeable decline in combat activity. With the spring thaw, heavy snow melt in the mountains results in flooding, mudslides and muddy or washed-out roads and paths, also limiting the level of combat. The combat season, then, for much of the border area traditionally runs from late March through October — although a new U.S. strategy could call for sustained pressure during the winter months.

The mountains also limit the use of helicopters, which become more difficult to operate with maximum payloads at higher eleva-tions, in the hot summer weather and through overcast skies. Yet the distribution of NATO forces in Afghanistan makes helicopters a coveted asset in theater. Even the most basic military maneuvers are extremely taxing in the high and rugged border areas, which also afford a distinct advantage to locals who are acclimated to the altitude and intimately familiar with the terrain.

To the east of the most heavily traveled border region are Pakistan's FATA, NWFP and Balochistan province. Covering nearly 40,000 square miles, the FATA and NWFP together are larger than the group of northeastern U.S. states known as New England (minus Maine); yet with almost 20 million people, the FATA/NWFP area is more populous than all of New England and has a much higher population density. NWFP is very nearly three times as densely pop-ulated as all of New England.

This density offers exceptional human camouflage for Taliban and al Qaeda fighters and their core leadership as well as jihadist actors of various other stripes. Offering infiltration routes and sanctuaries (where someone like Osama bin Laden or Mullah Omar can remain

PAKTIKA-WAZIRISTAN BORDER CORRIDOR

TURKMENISTAN

IRAN

AFGHANISTAN

Arabian Sea

PAKISTAN

Kabul

Islamabad

CHINA

INDIA

Afghanistan/Pakistan border

Potential roads/routes of travel for Taliban and al Qaeda

Balochistan

Federally Administered Tribal Areas

Khyber-Pakhtunkhwa (formerly NWFP)

Paktika Province

Gowmal

Sarobi

Orgun-E

Margha

Bormol

Mangretay

Gayan

Bibi

Shkin

Chaprai

Khuni Qala

Dabar Miami

Ghazlamai

Wana

Federally Administered Tribal Areas

Tatai

AFGHANISTAN

PAKISTAN

0 mi   10

undiscovered despite the best efforts of the Bush administration), the border region is receptive to the Islamist cause and has been since the Soviet intervention in Afghanistan in 1979. The FATA was the staging ground for the Afghan mujahideen resistance, and the multinational Islamist fighters who poured into the FATA and NWFP — supported by the United States as well as Pakistan — were seen by the local Pashtun tribes as noble guardians against Russian aggression. From tribal cultures themselves, many of these foreign fighters eventually began to marry into the local tribes and establish roots in the region.

Cultural Landscape

Given the population density of Pakistan border provinces, the cultural landscape is a crucial consideration for military operations along the border. In the days of the British Empire, London left what is now known as the FATA autonomous because the region was considered hostile and ungovernable, due not only to the rugged terrain but also to the intense tribal loyalty among the people. The occasional imperial intervention never ended well. The region retained its autonomy when Pakistan became first the Dominion of Pakistan in 1947 and then the Islamic Republic of Pakistan in 1956. And the region remains autonomous to this day.

Although the two main Pakistani Pashtun areas are often lumped together on military maps, there are significant differences between the FATA and NWFP. While the FATA have enjoyed a great deal of autonomy, NWFP is a full-fledged part of the Pakistani federation. Like all provinces in Pakistan, NWFP is ruled by a chief minister who heads the provincial legislature and a governor appointed by Islamabad. In contrast, the FATA has been ruled directly by Islamabad through political agents working with the tribal leaders — a system that has broken down with the rise of the Pakistani Taliban, who seek to establish an Islamist state in the Pashtun areas. Because residents are so hostile to outsiders, security in the FATA is enforced mainly by paramilitary organizations like the Pakistani Frontier Corps, which recruits locally and serves as the tip of the spear for regular-army operations in the region.

For many regional inhabitants, their support of the mujahideen did not end in 1989 when the Soviets withdrew from Afghanistan. The battle-hardened foreign fighters, many of whom were not allowed to return to their native countries, stayed on to fight the communist Afghan regime, which was brought down in 1992. Amid the factional infighting that ensued, the Taliban emerged in 1994 and took control of Kabul in 1996. Until the 9/11 attacks, foreign fighters flocked to Afghanistan — often through northwestern Pakistan. When the Taliban regime withdrew in the face of the U.S. onslaught — declining to fight — the FATA was the easy and obvious fallback position.

In 2004, under pressure from the Bush administration, the Pakistani army began addressing the growing Taliban/al Qaeda issue in the FATA, resulting in heavy fighting with intermittent peace agreements that fell apart under the weight of a maturing Pakistani insurgency. It is a landscape that has grown only more hostile to government rule and U.S. influence in recent years, and civilian casualties caused by UAV airstrikes and cross-border raids into Pakistan are not winning any hearts and minds.

But it is also a complex landscape in which many different ethnic, tribal, ideological, religious and nationalistic loyalties collide. While an assortment of disaffected tribes host a variety of Islamist militants in the FATA and NWFP, a host of other tribes and militant groups remain loyal to and under the control of the Pakistani state. Indeed, in Islamabad's eyes, the border areas are home to both "good" Taliban and "bad" Taliban — the former focused on the fight in Afghanistan, the latter on the insurgency in Pakistan.

The seven agencies of the FATA are Bajaur, Mohmand, Khyber, Orakzai, Kurram, North Waziristan and South Waziristan. Bajaur, with Khar as its capital, is the northernmost agency. To the north and east, Bajaur borders the NWFP districts of Dir and Malakand — two areas where STRATFOR believes the apex leadership of al Qaeda prime is likely hiding. There are three main tribes in Bajaur: the Utman Khel, Tarkalanri and Mamund. The Pakistani army is currently engaged in a major operation against Taliban elements in Bajaur, which also has experienced a number of airstrikes by U.S. UAVs, at least one of which was reportedly targeting Ayman al-Zawahiri, al Qaeda's number two.

In Mohmand agency, the key tribes are the Mohmand, Musa Khel, Daud Khel, Mero Khel, Tarak Zai, Safi, Utman Khel and Halim Zais. Al-Zawahiri is married to a native of this agency and is thought to visit the agency frequently. Mohmand made the headlines June 11 when a U.S. airstrike struck a Frontier Corps outpost and killed 11 Pakistani troops including a mid-level officer.

Khyber agency contains the crucial Khyber Pass, one of the most important roads across the Afghan-Pakistani frontier. It is the main artery connecting Peshawar to Kabul and passes through the border town of Torkham. Because of this artery, Khyber is the most developed agency in the tribal belt. It is inhabited by four tribes — the Afridi, Shinwari, Mullagori and Shimani. Until fairly recently, the insurgent Pakistani Taliban had not been a problem in Khyber, but there are now at least three Taliban factions challenging the writ of the central government.

Orakzai is the only FATA agency that does not border Afghanistan. It is sandwiched between Khyber and Kurram agencies and NWFP's Peshawar, Nowshera, Kohat and Hangu districts. Its capital, Darra Adam Khel, is the site of a well-known and illegal regional arms bazaar. The Orakzai tribes consist of two major groups: the original Orakzai and the migrant Hamsaya. The security situation in Orakzai is not as bad as it is in other parts of the FATA, but there are still issues with the Taliban in Orakzai, and some sectarian strife has spilled over from neighboring Kurram agency.

Kurram is the second largest tribal region in the FATA. The agency has a significant Shiite population and has been the scene of fierce sectarian clashes. The agency also has a significant jihadist presence. It is home to a number of tribes: the Turi, Bangash, Parachamkani, Massozai, Alisherzai, Zaimusht, Mangal, Kharotai, Ghalgi and Hazara.

North Waziristan is inhabited by the Utmanzai Wazirs, Daurs and other smaller tribes such as the Gurbaz, Kharsins, Saidgis and Malakshi Mehsuds. In the days of the British, tribesmen from this area rallied around Mirzali Khan, who was later given the title of the Faqir of Ipi. Under him, jihad was declared against the British, and his huge lashkar (force) remained at war with the British until Pakistan gained its independence in 1947. In late 2005, elements of the Pakistani Taliban declared the establishment of an Islamic emirate in North Waziristan, which is the headquarters of pro-Islamabad Afghan Taliban commander Jalaluddin Haqqani, whose house was hit by missiles fired from U.S. UAVs Sept. 9 and a large number of his relatives were killed.

The southernmost agency of the tribal belt is South Waziristan, in which the two main tribes are the Mehsuds and Wazirs. South Waziristan was the first part of the FATA to be the target of the Pakistani military operations that began in 2004. The Pakistani government has tried to undermine the power of the most prominent Pakistani Taliban leader, Baitullah Mehsud, and his Waziristan-based Tehrik-i-Taliban Pakistan movement through rival Taliban warlord Maulvi Nazir, who is pro-central government. Mehsud, also directly linked to al Qaeda, is known to have a large number of foreign fighters in South Waziristan, especially Uzbeks. Islamabad attempted to restore order through a number of deals with militants in the agency — all of which have fallen apart. Security forces are now facing stiff resistance from the militants.

Logistics

Against this border backdrop of mountainous terrain, weather and internal and external strife must flow supplies for Western forces as well as Taliban and foreign jihadists. As U.S. forces conduct cross-border raids in Pakistan, heightening tensions between Pakistan and the United States, U.S. and NATO military operations in Afghanistan depend heavily on logistical routes from Pakistan. Somewhere between 80 and 90 percent of U.S./NATO supplies arrive in Afghanistan from Pakistan in massive convoys with civilian truck drivers. On the Pakistan side of the border, convoy security is provided by the Pakistani army. The convoys cross the border on two roads from Pakistan — one east of Kabul, the other east of Kandahar. Especially on the northern route, these convoys transit the very heart of the FATA and NWFP and are frequently attacked by bandits and Taliban and jihadist fighters. The bazaars of border cities such as Quetta and Peshawar are awash in cheap, plundered U.S. and NATO military goods.

The connection to the ocean through the port of Karachi is extremely important for U.S. and NATO logistics in Afghanistan, as is the continued flow of fuel from Pakistani refineries. Alternative routes from the north and northeast are used for the remaining 10 to 20 percent of supplies, but these routes are not as established or as efficient as those through Pakistan. They are also influenced by Russia, which, though not a decisive issue, has become an increasing concern since Moscow's assertiveness in Georgia. The infrastructure connecting Karachi to Kandahar, Kabul and the internal "Ring Road" that connects Afghanistan's major cities are by far the most efficient, established and heavily used logistical routes for NATO and U.S. forces in theater. The collapse of these routes would create an enormous logistical problem all but impossible to solve from the air for any length of time.

Challenges for Pakistan

Pakistan's military presence in the border areas — consisting of the Frontier Corps, other locally recruited paramilitary units and regular army troops — amounts to roughly 100,000 armed men.

These forces occupy small, scattered and isolated outposts attempting to cover hundreds of miles of rugged border terrain. They have little expectation of reinforcement and their own supply lines either are directly controlled by Taliban loyalists and foreign jihadists or are contingent on the goodwill of the tribal leaders in the territory the supply lines pass through — tribes that are struggling to balance the demands of Islamabad and the Taliban. Though the Pakistani army has deployed its own units to the region, it has little more in the way of reinforcements and already feels stretched thin in the east, where it sits opposite qualitatively and quantitatively superior Indian forces.

Beyond the myriad conflicting loyalties along Pakistan's western border, perhaps the most persistent problem is posed by the Directorate for Inter-Services Intelligence (ISI), the country's main intelligence agency. The ISI played a key role in the rise of transnational jihadism in the first place by cultivating Islamist militants for its own strategic purposes in Afghanistan and Kashmir. Pakistan perceived the U.S. lack of interest in Afghanistan after the Soviet withdrawal as a green light for it to do as it pleased in Afghanistan. Meanwhile, al Qaeda pursued its own agenda, and many of Pakistan's own jihadist proxies became more and more autonomous. Eventually, the post-9/11 global security environment ruptured the ISI-jihadist relationship. More recently, the ISI appears to have lost control of many of its former proxies, although extensive ties remain. The current reality for Pakistan seems to be that, while it can establish a broad presence in the border areas with paramilitary forces in small outposts and ISI ties to the Taliban, the presence is rife with questionable loyalties, and the government's foothold along the border remains a very tenuous one.

In short, the Pakistani armed forces are simply not able to alter, in any meaningful way, the local dynamics on the border that underlay the growing domestic insurgency, much less combat the Taliban and foreign jihadist fighters who move back and forth across the border. To have any influence at all in Afghanistan, Islamabad has no choice but to use the Pashtun community — and the Taliban are the most potent force among the Afghan Pashtuns. But supporting these "good" Taliban in Afghanistan has strengthened the domestic "bad" Taliban who seek to establish an Islamist state on Pakistani soil. This is finally becoming an untenable situation for Islamabad.

Challenges for the U.S. and NATO

U.S. and NATO forces are stretched even thinner along the border than the Pakistanis are, and their efforts to stem the tide of fighters and supplies crossing the frontier from the Bajaur border town of Khar in the north to the Balochistan border town of Chaman to the south have largely failed. Western requirements for a military out-post are much higher in terms of defensibility, manning and access to supplies and timely reinforcement. And the U.S./NATO force in Afghanistan is already a lean one — 50,000 to 60,000 troops only now being meaningfully reinforced by the fledgling Afghan National Army (ANA) — with an overwhelming mission: secure all of Afghanistan, engage in heavy combat operations to the south, train the ANA and attempt to stem the Taliban/al Qaeda tide crossing the border.

While persistent UAV orbits help provide situational awareness, the rugged terrain makes it difficult to distinguish, from the air, guer-rillas and vehicles carrying supplies for the Taliban from civilians and their vehicles — and UAVs cannot replace foot patrols and interac-tion with the locals for intelligence gathering. UAV airstrikes have left enough innocent people dead to undermine Western legitimacy in the eyes of many locals on both sides of the border. Naturally, the problem also has been seized upon by al Qaeda and the Taliban for propaganda purposes. Meanwhile, the West is making few friends in the border areas as the United States continues to conduct overt and unilateral cross-border actions (often with collateral damage).

It is an extremely tough situation for the West — more daunt-ing, perhaps, than the challenges in Iraq. The ethnic and tribal com-plexities of the Afghan-Pakistani border, along with the deep roots of ultraconservative Islam in the region, make the ethno-sectarian strife among Iraq's Sunni, Shia and Kurds look uncomplicated. Add the logistical challenges of asserting military force along the Afghan-Pakistani border and Islamabad's lengthening laundry list of unten-able security problems, and the military challenges for the West seem almost insurmountable. The border territory is effectively controlled by tribal and militant leaders with conflicting if not incompatible loyalties — loyalties to those outside the Pakistani government, to those within it and, in many cases, to both sides. Islamabad vocally opposes U.S. violations of its territory and sovereignty and struggles to demonstrate to its people that it has their interests at heart, even though it must maintain the U.S. relationship for essential military aid and economic support.

These issues present profound challenges for both Washington and Islamabad, but the United States must find a way to address the border situation if it hopes to turn the tables in Afghanistan. Pakistan is losing ground to the Taliban on its own territory and cannot address the problem on its own.

A Border Playbill: Militant Actors on the Afghan-Pakistani Frontier
Feb. 16, 2010

Over the course of the U.S./NATO mission in Afghanistan, much attention has been paid to the Afghan-Pakistani border, a very porous demarcation line transited at many points by hundreds, if not thousands, of people every day. The border area reaches north to the Hindu Kush and southwest into the arid Balochistan plateau. The border itself is poorly defined, cutting through mountain chains and ungoverned territory out of the reach of Islamabad and Kabul. In Pakistan, a large portion of the territory along its northwestern border — the Federally Administered Tribal Areas (FATA) — enjoys special autonomous status, in no small part because Islamabad has never been able to effectively extend its writ into this area and has, until just recently, never had the strategic need to do so.

The Durand Line, the actual demarcation that separates Afghanistan from Pakistan, was drawn by Great Britain in 1893 to form the border between British-owned India and Russia's sphere of influence in Afghanistan. When Pakistan was partitioned from India, it inherited the Durand Line and viewed the mountainous territory as a buffer zone from Afghanistan. However, Afghanistan has never formally recognized the line as an administrative border and, over the ages, has considered it not a buffer but an invasion route. Before the Durand Line, regional warlords based in what is now Afghanistan would come down from the mountains to invade the Indus River valley in what then belonged to India. In fact, the Mughal dynasty that ruled India from approximately 1526 to 1707 came from Afghanistan, as did its predecessor, the Sultanate of Delhi.

Additionally, the ethnicity of the population along the border is mostly Pashtun, a largely tribal society that shares connections across the border and has a history that far predates any national partitions. The modern state system of territorial control and boundaries simply does not work here. Instead, the control of territory is much more byzantine, based on intricate understandings that are very local and fluid. Successfully navigating in such a region requires an intimate knowledge of ever-changing local politics. The Afghan-Pakistani border area, then, can be seen as its own region, with allegiances and interests that supersede those of far-away, centralized governments in Kabul and Islamabad and pay little heed to an official line drawn on a map.

During the 1979-1989 Soviet war in Afghanistan, Pakistan used the fluidity of the border region to its advantage. Along with the CIA and the Saudi General Intelligence Directorate, the Pakistanis used the FATA as a staging ground for conducting operations in Afghanistan against the Soviets, running people and supplies over a border that the Soviets were unable to control. Toward the end of the war, Pakistan started seeing competition from Arab-led international militants for influence in Afghanistan when the Soviets pulled out. These Arab fighters established relations with local Afghan fighters and became what is now al Qaeda prime. Following the 9/11 attacks and the U.S./NATO invasion of Afghanistan, al Qaeda pulled back into the borderland between Afghanistan and Pakistan and has been hunkered down there ever since. The arrival of al Qaeda on Pakistan's frontier turned the tables on Islamabad, making the borderland more of a liability than an asset.

The United States was quick to enlist Pakistan as an ally in its war against al Qaeda and its supporters in the border area. After the U.S./ NATO invasion of Afghanistan, and as part of a deal with the United States, then-Pakistani President Gen. Pervez Musharraf largely disassociated Pakistan from the Afghan Taliban and later banned a number of Pakistani militant groups that it had been supporting. Turning on these groups triggered a militant backlash that has led to the current insurgency challenging Islamabad.

However, Pakistan continues to have the best networks for understanding the realities on the ground in Afghanistan. With little hope or capability of establishing a human intelligence network of its own in the area, the United States has relied on Pakistan's Inter-Services Intelligence (ISI) directorate for intelligence on the region and the people who inhabit it. The ISI, in turn, relies on its network of jihadist forces that it created to give the region some sense of cohesion and project power in Afghanistan (though in the last three years a large portion of that network has been waging war against the Pakistani state).

Major Militant Players

The larger jihadist community in the border area consists of militant groups in Afghanistan and Pakistan that have carved out territorial niches, many of which overlap political boundaries and each other. For the sake of simplicity, we have broken militants operating along the border into three main groups: the Afghan Taliban led by Mullah Mohammad Omar, the Tehrik-i-Taliban Pakistan (TTP), whose leadership is currently in flux, and the Afghan Taliban regional command in eastern Afghanistan, led by the Haqqani family. Dozens of other groups operate along the border, but few of them are able to claim any significant territorial control or play as meaningful a role in the fighting as the three main groups. They contribute fighters and materiel when they can, and occasionally they are credited for attacks in Afghanistan and Pakistan. But the three main groups are the most powerful when it comes to influencing events in the border region and, as such, are the focus of Western and Pakistani military efforts.

The map on page 107 is a very general representation of the situation on the ground, based on a limited amount of credible information from Afghan, Pakistani and Western military sources. Territorial control in the border region is difficult to illustrate, since such sources view the terrain and define control in terms of political boundaries, when in reality such boundaries are not so clear-cut.

Before discussing the various groups that operate in the Afghan-Pakistani border region, we should outline the geographic differences along the border between north and south. The northern border area is defined by difficult-to-access mountain ranges that have made this area almost impossible for any kind of central government to control. Conversely, the southern border is a plateau, making up the province of Balochistan on the Pakistani side and Nimroz, Helmand and Kandahar provinces on the Afghan side.

On the Pakistani side, the northern border is dominated by the FATA and a stretch of the North-West Frontier Province (NWFP) to the north. Islamabad has very little presence in the FATA, and while the area belongs to Pakistan in name, much of it is under the de facto control of local tribal warlords. The Pakistani military has managed to take control of an area in South Waziristan, but it remains to be seen how effectively the military can control Pakistani Taliban elements in other FATA districts like North Waziristan, Orakzai, Kurram, Khyber, Mohmand and Bajaur. As a general rule, the Pakistani Taliban are stronger the farther west one goes in the Pashtun areas of northwestern Pakistan. The farther east one goes, the more the central government has a presence.

This devolution of power to the tribal leaders in the FATA, many of whom are now militant commanders, allows for much more unmonitored cross-border traffic through the mountains. This fluidity allows militants fighting Western forces in eastern Afghanistan to work much more closely with militants in the FATA. In a region where few roads exist, inhabitants are very comfortable negotiating

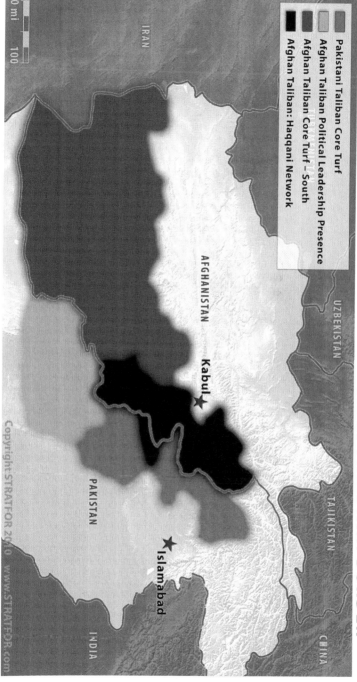

MILITANT PRESENCE ALONG THE AFGHAN-PAKISTANI BORDER

Pakistani Taliban Core Turf
Afghan Taliban Political Leadership Presence
Afghan Taliban Core Turf – South
Afghan Taliban: Haqqani Network

0 mi   100

IRAN

AFGHANISTAN

UZBEKISTAN

TAJIKISTAN

CHINA

Kabul

PAKISTAN

Islamabad

INDIA

Copyright STRATFOR 2010   www.STRATFOR.com

mountain paths that were created over centuries of use. Whether they are large enough for a motorized vehicle or barely wide enough for a human on foot, these primitive arteries inextricably link the FATA to its neighboring provinces in Afghanistan.

It is unreasonable to expect the Pakistani military to patrol all of these paths — even if they could effectively do that, locals have a superior knowledge of the landscape and can quickly adopt alternative routes. The unregulated, unmonitored flow of goods and people across the Afghan-Pakistani border in the north means that counter-insurgency efforts on either side of the border are going to be frustrated by the cross-border support of the insurgent network.

The dominant militant group in the FATA is the TTP, which is a largely indigenous force that has been escalating its insurgent activity against Islamabad since 2007. The group also boasts a large number of foreign fighters from the Arabian Peninsula and Central Asia (e.g., Uzbekistan). Opposite the FATA is the Afghan Taliban regional command in eastern Afghanistan, led by the Haqqani network. This network — the single largest militant grouping within the Afghan Taliban movement — has a significant presence in the FATA that supports operations against Western troops in Afghanistan.

The TTP emerged as a result of the relocation of al Qaeda from Afghanistan into northwest Pakistan, Islamabad's alignment with Washington in the war against the jihadists and Pakistan's inability to balance its commitment to the United States with its need to maintain influence in Afghanistan. The TTP has carried out attacks in Pakistan's core and has been escalating the frequency of its attacks since the security operation against militants holed up in Islamabad's Red Mosque in 2007. In recent months it has spread its presence down to Sindh province and Pakistan's strategic city of Karachi. The TTP has also been weakened, having lost its principal sanctuary in South Waziristan and at least two of its principal leaders.

In October 2009, the Pakistani military launched a ground operation in South Waziristan to deny the TTP sanctuary and the capability to train and deploy fighters into Pakistan's core. The success of this mission remains to be seen as the long-term challenges of actually holding territory and controlling and preventing militant forces from returning become all too obvious. The rugged geography and distance from Islamabad (exacerbated by poor infrastructure) will certainly play to the advantage of the local insurgents.

Separate from the TTP are militant commanders such as Hafiz Gul Bahadur and Maulvi Nazir, who operate in North and South Waziristan respectively, drawing support from foreign fighters and providing support to Afghan Taliban elements west of the border. These are Pakistani Taliban forces that are focused on the Afghan front and are not interested in fighting Islamabad. At times, the Pakistani military has tried to reach neutrality agreements with such commanders in an effort to isolate the TTP. Although they have not always been successful, current efforts to manage these actors are bearing fruit, and the neutrality understandings seem to be holding.

To the southwest in Pakistan is the province of Balochistan, which is far different from the FATA in the sense that it is a full-fledged province of Pakistan with multiple layers of governance, including a strong federal presence. Northeast Balochistan province is slightly different, in that it has a large Pashtun population, which links the province ethnically to the FATA, NWFP and neighboring Afghanistan. This section of the province does provide limited opportunities to militant groups operating in the border region.

However, the Afghan Taliban in southern Afghanistan, adjacent to Balochistan, do not rely as much on the border area as Taliban elements to the north do. Southern Afghanistan, particularly the province of Kandahar, just across the border from Quetta (the provincial capital of Balochistan), is the birthplace of the Afghan Taliban movement and remains its stronghold. Mullah Omar's Taliban movement originally began in Kandahar in response to the lawlessness brought about under Soviet rule and the resulting civil war after the Soviets left. The Taliban eventually expanded to rule 90 percent of Afghanistan but were pushed back to their southern heartland after the U.S./NATO invasion.

Unlike in northern Afghanistan, where Western forces are constantly applying pressure to Taliban forces, the Taliban continue to control large swaths of territory in the south. When foreign forces do conduct offensives in the area, Taliban forces can very easily melt into the local countryside. While Taliban activity is concentrated closer to the border in the north, the border has less strategic value for the Taliban in the south, in part because the insurgents continue to control southern territory that Western military forces have been unable to wrest away. Thus they are able to operate much more openly there and do not have the same need to escape across a border when the pressure is applied.

Moreover, the Taliban's territorial control in southern Afghanistan does not extend to the border, as it does in the north. The Taliban are largely a Pashtun phenomenon, with the most reach among Afghanistan's Pashtun population, which does not extend to the border in the south. For the Afghan Taliban, fleeing across the southern border is a long and harrowing trip to a region of Pakistan kept under close watch by the Pakistani military — far different from the situation in the north.

The Afghan Taliban, however, do maintain a presence in Pakistan. Their political leadership is believed to be somewhere in the greater Quetta area, where they have sought sanctuary from Western military forces in Afghanistan. They do not directly cause violence in Pakistan, though, and since they are in Balochistan, an official Pakistani province, they have not been subjected to the kind of pressure from U.S.-operated unmanned aerial vehicle (UAV) strikes that are frequently conducted against militants in the FATA. Afghan Taliban leaders in Balochistan do not cross back and forth over the border but remain much more sedentary, blending in with fellow ethnic Pashtuns and staying away from border areas where Western and Afghan forces have much more freedom to target them.

The largest Taliban regional command structure under Mullah Omar is led by the Haqqani family in eastern Afghanistan (essentially serving as the Afghan Taliban's eastern "wing"). The Haqqani family has been a powerful force in eastern Afghanistan since well before the Taliban started their rise to power. The Haqqani family also teamed up with al Qaeda and foreign militants in the region before the Taliban did. They assimilated under Mullah Omar's rule when the Taliban took over in the 1990s, but because of the group's special status, the Haqqani family was able to maintain a large degree of autonomy in conducting its operations. The Haqqani network also has a significant presence in the FATA — especially in North Waziristan — and has frequently been the target of coordinated U.S. UAV strikes there.

A Fluid Insurgency

None of these groups is monolithic. Just as the border region is fragmented in ways that make it difficult for central governments to control it, so are its main insurgent groups, which do not have clear, hierarchical control over their territories. Rather, they are engaged in a medieval web of allegiances in which various factions are either united against a common enemy or quarreling over territorial control.

In Pakistan, we saw a tumultuous struggle over leadership of the TTP after its leader, Baitullah Mehsud, was killed by a suspected U.S.-operated UAV strike. We also saw independent warlords like Maulvi Nazir reach oral neutrality "agreements" (more like informal understandings) with the Pakistani government to make it easier for the Pakistani military to move into South Waziristan during its offensive there. Similarly, in Afghanistan, we saw regional commanders continue to carry out suicide bombings in civilian areas despite calls from Mullah Omar to limit civilian casualties by requiring approval for such acts. The Afghan Taliban appear to be unified because they face a common enemy, the United States and NATO in Afghanistan, just as the various elements of the Pakistani Taliban seem to be in concert in their fight against Islamabad. But these groups must be pragmatic in order to survive in a geography that prevents any single power from dominating it completely — and this requires shifting alliances quickly and often, depending on who offers the most benefit for the group at any given point.

Any insurgent force usually has two kinds of enemies at the same time: the foreign occupying or indigenous government force it is trying to defeat, and other revolutionary entities with which it is competing for power. While making inroads against the former, the Taliban have not yet resolved the issue of the latter. It is not so much that various insurgent factions and commanders are in direct competition with each other; the problem for the Taliban, reflecting the rough reality that the country's mountainous terrain imposes on its people, is the disparate nature of the movement itself. Its many factions share few objectives beyond defeating Western and Afghan and Pakistani (in the case of the TTP and its allies) government forces.

Far from a monolithic movement, the term "Taliban" encompasses everything from old hard-liners of the pre-9/11 Afghan regime to small groups that adopt the name as a "flag of convenience," whether they are Islamists devoted to a local cause or criminals wanting to obscure their true objectives. The multifaceted and often confusing character of the Taliban "movement" actually creates a layer of protection around it. The United States has admitted that it does not have the nuanced understanding of the Taliban's composition necessary to identify potential moderates who can be separated from the hard-liners.

The main benefits of waging any insurgency usually boil down to the following: Insurgents operate in squad- to platoon-sized elements, have light or nonexistent logistical tails, are largely able to live off the land or the local populace, can support themselves by seizing weapons and ammunition from weak local police and isolated outposts and can disperse and blend into the environment whenever they confront larger and more powerful conventional forces. The border area between Pakistan and Afghanistan is ideal terrain for insurgents to play off of three national powers in the region; militants fighting against Islamabad can seek refuge in Afghanistan, and militants fighting the Afghan government can just as easily seek sanctuary in Pakistan. U.S. and other Western forces are then left with the challenge of distinguishing between and fighting the various factions, all the while recognizing (for the most part) a political boundary their adversaries completely ignore.

Conflicting Interests

Of course, the two major actors in the border area are the United States and Pakistan. Pakistan's objective in the region is to eliminate domestic threats that challenge the state and national security. This objective puts Pakistani forces squarely at odds with the TTP and its allies that have a sizable presence in the FATA, and this has increased attacks across a larger part of Pakistan over the past two years.

However, it is in Pakistan's interest to maintain influence in neighboring Afghanistan in order to shape the political environment and ensure that pro-Islamabad factions hold power there. This means that Islamabad largely supports the Afghan Taliban led by Mullah Omar, including his key subordinates, the Haqqanis, as well as the Taliban assets and allies in Pakistan who support them without stirring up trouble for Islamabad. Other examples of these "good Taliban" are the factions led by Maulvi Nazir, Hafiz Gul Bahadur and other lesser commanders in the FATA.

Meanwhile, the United States is focused on weakening the Afghan Taliban elements and their central leader, Mullah Omar, in order to weaken the network of support that allowed foreign jihadists to mount transnational terror campaigns from Afghanistan. Although this strategy goes against key Pakistani interests in the region, recent statements by U.S. Central Command chief Gen. David Petraeus indicate that the United States is shoring up support for Pakistan. On Feb. 3, Petraeus lauded Pakistan's counterinsurgency efforts over the past year and suggested that the United States will rely on Pakistan to negotiate any kind of peace deal with Taliban elements that the United States finds agreeable. This would put Pakistan in a solid position to have more influence over the outcome of events in its neighboring country.

The fact remains that the Afghan-Pakistani border is not a geographical reality. It is an unnatural political overlay on a fragmented landscape that is virtually impossible for a central government to control. In peaceful times, regional powers can afford to ignore it and let the tribal actors tend to their own business. When the stakes are raised in a guerrilla war, however, the lack of control creates a haven and a highway for insurgents. As the United States continues to have a presence in Afghanistan, it will not be able to control the border lands without the assistance of Pakistan, which naturally has its own interests in the region. Negotiations among the United States, Pakistan, Afghanistan and other nearby powers are challenging enough. Factor in an assortment of disparate actors that exist in a separate space and the challenges grow even greater.

CHAPTER 4: PAKISTAN

Anatomy of the ISI
Aug. 11, 2008

Pakistan's Directorate of Inter-Services Intelligence (ISI), the country's main intelligence agency, played a key role in the rise of transnational jihadism by cultivating Islamist militants for its own strategic purposes in Afghanistan and Kashmir. The Pakistanis — especially the ISI — perceived the United States' lack of interest in Afghanistan after the Soviet withdrawal as a green light for them to do as they pleased in the country, and in neighboring India. In the meantime, al Qaeda was pursuing its own agenda, and many of Pakistan's own proxies were becoming more and more autonomous. Finally, the post-9/11 global security environment ruptured the ISI-jihadist relationship. Much more recently, the ISI appears to have lost control of many of its former proxies as well as itself.

A growing Taliban movement assuming control of various parts of Pashtun-dominated northwestern Pakistan, increasing U.S. unilateral operations against al Qaeda and Taliban elements in the same area and Islamist militant attacks in neighboring Afghanistan and India, all have one common denominator: the ISI.

Suicide bomb attacks — mostly against Pakistan's security services — and the erosion of the writ of the government in Pakistan's tribal belt and many areas of the North-West Frontier Province are taking place because the ISI's former assets are able to use their ties within the directorate to sustain their operations. Jihadists fighting the Pakistani state are able to exploit both the Pakistani army's inability and/or unwillingness to completely sever ties with Islamist militants and the significant presence of Islamist sympathizers within the ISI.

Meanwhile, the United States — after long suspecting elements within the ISI and other parts of the military of colluding with al Qaeda and Taliban militants — has moved toward taking overt unilateral action against Pakistan-based jihadist forces. The official manner in which Washington, including President George W. Bush himself, has come out questioning the ISI in recent weeks is unprecedented. Until now, the Bush administration never directly criticized the directorate and other institutions within the army, relying instead on media leaks to put pressure on the Pakistanis to rein in the ISI. Should things get out of hand, it is not beyond the realm of possibility that Washington could officially designate the ISI a terrorism-supporting entity (along the lines of the October 2007 U.S. executive order against Iran's Revolutionary Guard Corps).

At a time when the Pakistani state is trying to contain a runaway insurgency on the domestic front as well as maintain its status as a frontline ally in the U.S. war against Islamist militants, there is evidence implicating the ISI in large-scale attacks in both Afghanistan and India. The fact that Pakistan is the target of Islamist militants and can still commission attacks in both its neighboring countries speaks volumes about the nebulous nature of the ISI-jihadist nexus. While the intelligence service has clearly lost control of a significant number of militant Islamists, there are others that it still controls.

The jihadists never were a monolithic entity, but over time the ISI also has become an extremely complex organization fraught with internal contradictions. As with any other foreign intelligence service, its opaque nature creates conditions that are ripe for operations that might not necessarily have official sanction. Exacerbating this situation is the fact that the Pakistani state lacks any institutional checks that could help maintain oversight over ISI operations.

In addition to being an institution within the country's military establishment, the ISI also plays a key role in domestic politics — keeping the country's political parties in line — which gives it further immunity from any oversight. While it has kept civilian forces and ethno-nationalist movements under wraps, the ISI as a body has been compromised by the relationship it has cultivated with Islamist militant groups over the last three decades or so.

The Pre-Islamism Years

The ISI was created in 1948 by Maj. Gen. William Cawthorne, the British Deputy Chief of Staff of the Pakistani army. It was designed to address the intelligence failures of the existing directorate, Military Intelligence (MI), during the 1948 India-Pakistan War due to the lack of coordination among the three armed services. Given the political turmoil between 1948 and 1958, the ISI did not really gain prominence until the first military coup in 1958, which brought to power Gen. Ayub Khan. He ruled the country for more than a decade with the ISI as a key instrument of his regime. Thus, even before it was able to fulfill its original mandate (foreign intelligence), the ISI was sucked into the vortex of Pakistan's turbulent domestic political landscape.

During this period, the ISI became heavily involved in internal politics to sustain the president's regime and the military's dominance over the state even after Ayub Khan — who assumed the rank of field marshal — stepped down as military chief to consolidate his presidency. This could, to a great degree, help explain the ISI's dismal performance during the 1965 India-Pakistan war. Nonetheless, it was during the Ayub Khan years that the ISI established its primacy over MI and the civilian Intelligence Bureau (IB).

By the time Ayub Khan was forced out of office in 1969 and army chief Gen. Yahya Khan took over, the ISI had its hands full with domestic political upheaval as opposed to external threats. After the victory of the East Pakistan-based Awami League (AL) in the 1970 elections and Yahya Khan's refusal to hand power to AL leader

Sheikh Mujibur Rahman, civil war broke out between the western and eastern sides of the country, and the ISI was engaged in trying to crush the Bengali rising.

India's intervention in the civil war led to Pakistan's defeat in what has come to be known as the 1971 war. In the aftermath of the war, the country's first democratic leader, President (later Prime Minister) Zulfikar Ali Bhutto, tried to rein in the ISI by appointing Lt. Gen. Ghulam Jilani Khan as its head. Jilani Khan led the directorate for seven years. But even Bhutto increased the agency's domestic role, especially regarding the operation to put down the Baloch insurgency in 1974.

Cold War and Islamism

Another coup in 1977 that ousted Bhutto and brought to power pro-Islamist army chief Gen. Mohammed Zia-ul-Haq, along with Soviet intervention in Afghanistan in 1979, led to the ISI's long relationship with militant Islamist actors. For the next decade, the ISI — first under Gen. Akhtar Abdur Rahman (1980-87) and then Lt. Gen. Hamid Gul (1987-89) — with the help of the CIA and the Saudi General Intelligence Presidency (GIP) backed Islamist fighters to combat Soviet troops supporting the communist People's Democratic Party of Afghanistan (PDPA) government in Kabul. It was under the leadership of Abdur Rahman and Gul that Islamism crept into the body of the ISI.

The war against the Soviets was the culmination of the ISI's attempts to defeat ethno-nationalism among the Pashtuns living on both sides of the Durand Line by supporting Islamism as a rival ideology. Thus, the ISI defeated left-wing secular Pashtun national-ism but in the process helped the rise of militant Islamism, which, combined with the conservative tribal Pashtun culture, emerged as a much more formidable challenge.

As the Soviet army was pulling out of Afghanistan, al Qaeda's roots were being planted by Arab fighters who had participated in the war against the Soviets. Osama bin Laden and his legion of fighters had developed a close relationship with the ISI during the years when the ISI, CIA and GIP were focused on sustaining a proxy force that could counter the Soviets. But the ISI was more interested in the Afghan groups — specifically the Hizb-i-Islami of Gulbuddin Hekmatyar — because it wanted to see the pro-Soviet Mohammad Najibullah regime ousted and replaced with an Islamabad-friendly government that would provide Pakistan with "strategic depth" vis-à-vis India.

The hopes of the ISI (at this time led by overtly pro-jihadist chief Gul) to install a pro-Pakistani government in Kabul were dashed by the intra-Islamist civil war that broke out after the fall of the PDPA government. However, an indigenous rising had been taking shape in Indian-administered Kashmir since 1989, and the ISI used the resources it had developed during the Afghan war to begin aiding these groups and cultivating Kashmir-specific Islamist militant groups.

In the wake of the U.S. State Department's 1992 move to place Pakistan on its watch list of countries suspected of exporting terrorism, the Pakistanis tried to overhaul the ISI in order to avoid additional sanctioning. Lt. Gen. Javed Ashraf Qazi was appointed director-general of the ISI, and during his time (1993-1995) he took significant steps to restructure the organization, trying to move it away from its role of backing Islamists. Qazi introduced new guidelines and replaced quite a few people, but his efforts did not make much of a difference.

One of the reasons was that, while there was a genuine attempt to overhaul the ISI as a body, the directorate was still trying to establish a foothold for Islamabad in Kabul. The ISI achieved its goal of a pro-Pakistani government when it facilitated the rise of a new Pashtun Islamist movement called the Taliban, which had emerged out of the chaos of the early 1990s. Elements within the ISI also facilitated the return of Osama bin Laden and the al Qaeda leadership to Afghanistan in 1996, shortly after the Taliban seized the Afghan capital and bin Laden was forced to leave Sudan.

From the late 1980s onward, the ISI was also heavily involved on the home front, where it played a prominent role in the army's bid to check the power of the four civilian governments that ruled the country between 1988 and 1999. Meanwhile, the ISI and the Pakistani army were working to send Islamist militants into Indian Kashmir, a process that led to the short Kargil War in the summer of 1999 — the same year in which army chief Gen. Pervez Musharraf, a key figure in Pakistan's Kashmiri Islamist militant project, came to power in an October coup. Despite the reversal the Pakistanis faced in the Kargil War, the Taliban government in Kabul and its ability to continue backing Islamist militants in Kashmir kept the Pakistanis in a comfortable spot, with the Islamist militant proxies firmly under the ISI's control.

9/11 and its Aftermath

The events of Sept. 11, 2001, were a watershed in terms of forcing a behavioral change in the Pakistani state. The Musharraf government went from being an open supporter of the Taliban to (reluctantly) joining the United States in its war against al Qaeda and its host Taliban government. This is where the Pakistani state — especially the ISI — began losing control over the militants it had cultivated for more than a generation.

While there are those within the ISI who see the militants as valuable tools for achieving the state's foreign policy objectives, there are many others who "went native" and developed sympathies for these Islamist militants, even adopting the Islamist ideology of the people who were supposed to be their tools. The Pakistani military-intelligence complex was caught between the need to support the U.S. war against the jihadists and the need to cope with the rise of a hostile government in Afghanistan.

On one hand, the ISI was helping Washington capture and kill al Qaeda members; on the other, it was trying to maintain as much control as possible over the Taliban and other Islamist groups, which were enraged with Islamabad's decision to assist Washington. The ISI hoped its Kashmir operations would not be affected by the war against Islamist militants, but attacks on the Indian Parliament in December 2001 brought pressure from New Delhi. Musharraf was forced to ban many Kashmiri groups, which were subsequently allowed to reinvent themselves under different names.

Pakistan and India did step back from the brink of nuclear war in 2002, but the ISI lost control of many Kashmiri Islamist actors because of Musharraf's decision to halt operations in Kashmir. By that time, a trend had emerged in which several disgruntled Islamist actors left the Pakistani orbit and began aligning with al Qaeda, but many were still firmly under the control of the ISI and others were in-between.

As the Islamist militant universe was in flux, so was the ISI. The Pakistani government did make changes to the leadership of the organization, especially after attempts on Musharraf's life in December 2003. Nevertheless, it is very difficult to steer a whole organization with considerable power and influence in a completely different direction in a short period of time. While the directorate's leadership was busy trying to adjust to the post-9/11 operating environment, others within the middle and junior ranks continued with business as usual.

The next major blow to the ISI's control over the jihadists came when Musharraf — again under pressure from the United States — sent troops into the tribal belt, particularly the Waziristan region, in the spring of 2004. This move created problems for Pakistan's efforts to maintain influence over the Taliban, who had begun resurging in Afghanistan. Military operations that killed hundreds of people, including civilians, created resentment against the state in the area, played a key role in undermining the authority of the tribal elders through whom Islamabad maintained control over the Federally Administered Tribal Areas (FATA) and contributed to the rise of an indigenous Pakistani Taliban movement alongside the original Afghan Taliban movement.

Over the next two years, Pakistan signed at least three separate ill-fated peace agreements with the militants. Meanwhile, the United States had intensified its covert operations in the FATA in the hunt for al Qaeda and Taliban militants, especially in the form of Predator drone strikes. One such strike against a madrassa killed 82 people, mostly young seminary students.

This proved to be the trigger for a jihadist insurgency, led by top Pakistani Taliban commander Baitullah Mehsud, that struck against dozens of mostly army, police and intelligence personnel and facilities. The ability of the suicide bombers to strike with impunity against highly sensitive installations underscored the degree to which the ISI had lost control. Six months later, Musharraf's regime was overwhelmed with political movement after his decision to sack the country's chief justice. The Red Mosque operation July 3-11, 2007, was another turning point in that it intensified a nascent jihadist insurgency. Pakistani security forces attacking a mosque and contributing to the deaths of dozens of civilians (including women and children) — all of whom were viewed as demanding that "Islamic" law be implemented in a country that officially is an Islamic republic — gave the jihadists a major impetus to advance their campaign against the state. The raid on the mosque triggered a wave of suicide attacks targeting sensitive military installations, including those belonging to the ISI.

Musharraf's stepping down as army chief on Nov. 28, 2007, and his regime's replacement with a weak (albeit democratically elected) government that came to power in Feb. 18 elections, exacerbated the situation. And the state is too incoherent to combat Taliban forces that have taken control of significant chunks of territory in the NWFP. The stakeholders in the new civil-military setup realize the need to overhaul the ISI in order to successfully combat the jihadists at home and deal with mounting international pressure from all sides. But they lack the ability to engage in such a massive undertaking. Lack of public support, the fear of making matters worse and the possibility of losing their hold over the state have tied the hands of both the army and the intelligence leadership.

It is very difficult to make out who within the ISI is aiding Islamist militants of various shades. Given the attacks within the country, some ISI elements are definitely collaborating with the jihadists. It is also likely that some are pursuing their own objectives. And then there is the possibility that within the ISI the right hand does not know what the left hand is doing.

Other than some sketchy open-source material, information on the structure of the ISI is hard to come by. What is known is that beneath the director-general (who is of lieutenant-general rank) there are six major generals, who are also referred to as director-generals of their respective sub-units. Dozens of brigadiers report to these six two-stars, who in turn work with more than a hundred colonels who run various field/regional offices, along with thousands of junior officers. Though it is an army-dominated military organization, some 40 percent of the ISI's employees are civilians who are either retired from active military service or came through the civil service selection process. There are also many retired employees who continue to work with the directorate as contractors and consultants.

The ISI does have different departments that handle the various issues the service deals with, such as the Afghan and Kashmir cells. In addition to the bureaus involved in counterintelligence, signals intelligence and information technology, the ISI maintains an internal security branch that contains the political wing dealing with domestic political issues. The term "Islami wing," a reference to those elements who are either Islamist or pro-Islamist, has also become popularized in the local discourse.

Where it Goes From Here

The ISI evolved fairly rapidly, through domestic and regional crises and threats, into a much more powerful and dominant force in Pakistan, dealing with foreign intelligence, domestic security threats and military and political issues. Over time, it also took on a life of its own as a center of power in Pakistan — something that succeeding governments or regimes could not necessarily control but tried to manage. Attempts to rein in the ISI's power were met with resistance and mixed success and were put aside as new crises arose.

As the ISI evolved, it became the chief conduit for relations with Islamist militants — in part to mitigate their domestic impact but more to wield or manipulate them as foreign policy tools. At times, though, these relations with jihadists became the end rather than the means, as the ISI monolith continued along with minimal competent oversight or transparency.

Sometimes ISI/Islamist actions ran counter to state intent (as in the trigger for Kargil, for example) and exacerbated political crises and rivalries among various centers of power. At other times, the relationship was first seen as useful (support for the Taliban shored up Pakistan's buffer on its western border) and later seen as detrimental (support for the Taliban after 9/11). But the compartmentalized and opaque relations that had developed over time meant the ISI was not necessarily acting as a single unified entity, and operations and relations could and did contradict government policy and intent — even sometimes the intent of the ISI.

The current U.S.-Pakistani crisis is now shining a spotlight on the problems associated with trying to control an ISI that has, in many ways, taken on a life of its own — reaching into domestic and international politics, running its own operations and apparently blurring the lines between the idea of Islamists as a means to an end and Islamism as an end in itself.

Civilian rule in Pakistan has never taken root, and at the present time even the country's military establishment is having a hard time dealing with a rapidly deteriorating crisis of governance. That said, the military remains the only institution with the power to create change — but it can only do so if the country's intelligence system is overhauled. Even though it started out as a reluctant ally of Washington in the U.S.-jihadist war, Pakistan is now locked in its own existential struggle against religious extremism and terrorism, a struggle that simply cannot be won without an intelligence service free of jihadist links.

The fundamental need of the Pakistani state is to re-establish its waning writ, but it cannot do this without the help of a robust intelligence agency. And given the state's systemic inertia, the size of the

ISI and the government's fear of losing control over the state, the military's top brass are unable or unwilling to engage in a drastic overhaul of the directorate. Meanwhile, Pakistan is facing unprecedented internal political and security threats to its integrity that, if not mitigated soon, could erode the security and stability of the country to dangerous levels. Under these conditions, cleaning up an intelligence agency as powerful as the ISI can become a very messy affair, but the government officials who have made certain improvements over the past year cannot hope to regain control of their security situation and address international concerns unless they solve the chronic problems plaguing the ISI.

Afghanistan: Breaking Away from Pakistan's Influence
Sept. 9, 2008

A series of explosions destroyed a complex comprising a house and a madrassa in Pakistan's tribal belt Sept. 8. Six impacts were reported from what has been claimed to be a U.S. Air Force or CIA unmanned aerial vehicle. One villager claims that two drones fired three missiles apiece. The MQ-9 Reaper — a newer and larger version of the venerable RQ-1 Predator — regularly carries a combination of four AGM-114 Hellfire missiles and two 500-pound bombs fitted with either laser or Global Positioning System guidance kits.

The attack killed 23 people related to a very senior Taliban commander, Maulvi Jalaluddin Haqqani, who runs a major network of fighters and suicide bombers in Afghanistan managed by his son Sirajuddin. Another son, Badruddin, told media that his father and elder brother were not in the targeted house in the village of Dandi Darpakheil in the North Waziristan agency of the Federally Administered Tribal Areas (FATA) at the time of the attack. Those killed included one of Haqqani's wives, his sister-in-law, a sister, two nieces, eight grandchildren and another male relative. One of Haqqani's sons-in-law was wounded.

A U.S. attack targeting a jihadist figure close to Islamabad — and resulting in the deaths of several of his family members — could make matters worse in Pakistan. Islamabad is already dealing with an insurgency waged by jihadists gone rogue and growing anger among the public for increasing U.S. attacks in the country's northwest. The death of Haqqani's relatives could lead to Islamabad losing control over his group as well. A loss of control over key Pashtun militant figures and factions will lead Islamabad to completely lose the ability to shape Afghanistan.

The Haqqanis

Haqqani's importance can be gauged by reports that Afghan President Hamid Karzai in 2004 offered to make him prime minister in exchange for ending the insurgency. Haqqani established his Islamist militant credentials as a mujahideen commander during the 1980s war triggered by the Soviet intervention in Afghanistan. He was affiliated with Hizb-i-Islami (Younis Khalis Group) — one of the seven groups seeking to topple the Moscow-backed communist stratocracy in Kabul.

After the overthrow of the Marxist regime in 1992, Haqqani became justice minister in the first mujahideen government. Four years later, just before the Taliban captured Kabul, he joined Mullah Omar's movement and served as minister of borders and tribal affairs and as governor of Paktia province in the Taliban regime. He has had long-standing ties to Pakistani intelligence and, during the days of the Taliban, grew close to al Qaeda leader Osama bin Laden.

Since the fall of the Taliban regime in late 2001, Haqqani has been a major force behind the growing Taliban insurgency in Afghanistan, operating out of Pakistan's North Waziristan region and maintaining close ties with Islamabad. Haqqani's group falls into the category of jihadists that STRATFOR has identified as being close to both the Pakistanis and al Qaeda. He has been calling for a focus on operations in Afghanistan and is not in favor of the jihadist insurgency being waged against Pakistan by the Tehrik-i-Taliban Pakistan (TTP), led by Baitullah Mehsud. There have been reports that Haqqani's son Sirajuddin has been involved in mediation efforts between the TTP and Pakistani authorities.

More recently, U.S. Chairman of the Joint Chiefs of Staff Adm. Michael Mullen and CIA Deputy Director Steve Kappes, in a visit to Islamabad, gave the Pakistani military leadership evidence of the involvement of Pakistan's Inter-Services Intelligence (ISI) directorate in the bombing of the Indian Embassy in Kabul. A key piece of the evidence submitted to Pakistani army chief Gen. Ashfaq Kayani was communications between ISI officials and the Haqqani network, which is believed to have been behind the attack.

The Sept. 8 airstrike targeting the leadership of the Haqqani network suggests two things. First, the United States has made a significant breakthrough in terms of intelligence on the whereabouts of various Taliban and al Qaeda high-value targets. Second, and more important, Washington has now decided to go after jihadists who are still under Islamabad's control — an indicator of the increasing U.S. mistrust of Pakistan.

Islamabad's Limited Options

At a time when Islamabad is already having a hard time sorting out the "bad" Taliban from the "good" ones, U.S. unilateral action against jihadist elements still willing to work with Pakistan is a serious blow to Pakistan's struggle to regain influence in Afghanistan.

Ongoing overt U.S. operations, including the use of ground troops, have already put the Pakistani military under a lot of stress. Now, the Pakistani military has been forced to use some very strong language in speaking out against U.S. strikes to cater to a domestic audience angry over the violation of the country's sovereignty and the killing of noncombatants. Pakistani Maj. Murad Khan, a military spokesperson, told Iran's Press TV that Pakistani forces will act in self-defense if U.S. forces continue launching cross-border attacks, and Pakistan's air force chief told reporters that Pakistani forces need government permission to react to coalition attacks.

Pakistani authorities also engaged in some unorthodox moves when they briefly shut down the Torkham border crossing Aug. 6, preventing supplies from getting to NATO forces in Afghanistan. The Pakistanis said they could not guarantee the security of the shipments, given that their forces are battling three different militant groups in the region. That said, the Pakistanis kept open the main artery in Chaman — which links Pakistan to southern Afghanistan, the main theater of NATO operations against Taliban forces.

The Highway

The Pakistanis, however, were dealt a much larger blow. Indian Ambassador to Afghanistan Jayant Prasad, in an interview with Reuters published Sept. 8, announced the completion of a strategic road in southwestern Afghanistan built by Indian engineers that will allow the landlocked Afghans to reduce their dependency on Pakistan. The 135-mile road running from Delaram to Zaranj in Nimroz province was constructed by India's Border Roads Organization, a corps of engineers from the Indian army.

The road — the centerpiece of New Delhi's $1.1 billion reconstruction effort — opens up an alternate access route into Afghanistan. Currently, Afghanistan relies mostly on Pakistan for imports, with goods coming from Pakistani ports and then overland via the Khyber Pass. The new highway has been built upon an old road between two towns on the Iranian border that connects to a road to the Iranian port of Chabahar, a free-trade zone along the coast with the Gulf of Oman.

The starting point of the road is Delaram, which is situated on the "Garland Highway" linking Kabul, Kandahar, Herat, Mazar-i-Sharif and Kunduz. In a country without any major railway lines, this road serves as a national transportation system that has access to the outside world.

Islamabad views any Indian involvement in Afghanistan with suspicion and hostility. And this road — built by the Indian army and able to reduce Afghan dependency on Pakistan as an access route for trade with the outside world — is something that will hurt Pakistan's position. Pakistan has historically tried to establish a sphere of influence in Afghanistan in order to counter the threat Islamabad perceives from India.

Afghanistan's dependence on Pakistan for access to a port was one of the factors working in Islamabad's favor. But with Kabul gaining access to the Iranian port of Chabahar, the Pakistanis lose a key element of influence in the country. The construction of the highway only further undermines Pakistan's options as Islamabad faces blowback from the Taliban issue.

From Islamabad's point of view, the timing of the U.S. airstrike and the highway's completion could not have been worse, given the growing internal political, economic and security chaos in the country. And because it is unlikely that the new Pakistani government will be able to turn things around at home any time soon, it cannot do much to counter the United States' and India's moves to reduce Pakistani influence in Afghanistan.

The Perils of Using Islamism to Protect Pakistan's Core
Dec. 17, 2008

While Pakistan's boundaries encompass a large swath of land stretching from the peaks of the Himalayas to the Arabian Sea, the writ of the Pakistani state stops short of the country's mountainous northwestern frontier. The strip of arable land that hugs the Indus River in Punjab province is the Pakistani heartland, where the bulk of the country's population, industry and resources are concentrated.

129

For Pakistan to survive as a modern nation-state, it must protect this core at all costs.

But even in the best of circumstances, defending the Pakistani core and maintaining the integrity of the state are extraordinarily difficult tasks, mainly because of geography. The headwaters of the Indus River system are not even in Pakistan — the system actually begins in Indian-administered Kashmir. While Kashmir has been the focus of Indo-Pakistani military action in modern times, the area where Pakistan faces its most severe security challenge is the saddle of land between the Indus and the broader, more fertile and more populated Ganges River basin. The one direction in which it makes sense to extend Pakistani civilization as geography would allow takes Pakistan into direct and daily conflict with a much larger civilization: India. Put simply, geography dictates that Pakistan either be absorbed into India or fight a losing battle against Indian influence.

Controlling the Buffers

Pakistan must protect its core by imposing some semblance of control over its hinterlands, mainly in the north and west, where the landscape is more conducive to fragmenting the population than defending the country. The arid, broken highlands of the Balochistan plateau eventually leak into Iran to the southwest. To the north, in the North-West Frontier Province (NWFP), the Federally Administered Tribal Area (FATA), the Federally Administered Northern Area (FANA) and Azad Jammu and Kashmir (AJK), the terrain becomes more and more mountainous. But terrain in these regions still does not create a firm enough barrier to completely block invasion. To the southwest, a veritable Baloch thoroughfare parallels the Arabian Sea coast and crosses the Iranian-Pakistani border. To the northwest, the Pashtun-populated mountains are not so rugged that armies cannot march through them, as Alexander the Great, the Aryans and the Turks historically proved.

To control all these buffer regions, the Pakistani state must absorb masses of other peoples who do not conform to the norms of the

Indus core. Russia faces a similar challenge; its lack of geographic insulation from its neighbors forces it to expand to establish a buffer. But in Pakistan, the complications are far worse. Russia's buffers are primarily flat, which facilitates the assimilation of conquered peoples. Pakistan's buffers are broken and mountainous, which reinforces ethnic divisions among the regions' inhabitants — core Punjabis and Sindhis in the Indus Valley, Baloch to the west and Pashtuns to the north. And the Baloch and Pashtuns are spread out over far more territory than what comprises the Punjab-Sindh core.

Thus, while Pakistan has relatively definable boundaries, it lacks the ethnic and social cohesion of a strong nation-state. Three of the four major Pakistani ethnic groups — Punjabis, Pashtuns and Baloch — are not entirely in Pakistan. India has an entire state called Punjab, 42 percent of Afghanistan is Pashtun, and Iran has a significant Baloch minority in its Sistan-Balochistan province.

So the challenge to Pakistan's survival is twofold. First, the only route of expansion that makes any sense is along the fertile Indus River Valley, but that takes Pakistan into India's front yard. The converse is also true: India's logical route of expansion through Punjab takes it directly into Pakistan's core. Second, Pakistan faces an insurmountable internal problem. In its efforts to secure buffers, it is forced to include groups that, because of mountainous terrain, are impossible to assimilate.

The first challenge is one that has received little media attention of late but remains the issue for long-term Pakistani survival. The second challenge is the core of Pakistan's "current" problems: The central government in Islamabad simply cannot assert its writ into the outer regions, particularly in the Pashtun northwest, as well as it can at its core.

The Indus core could be ruled by a democracy — it is geographically, economically and culturally cohesive — but Pakistan as a whole cannot be democratically ruled from the Indus core and remain a stable nation-state. The only type of government that can realistically attempt to subjugate the minorities in the outer regions, who make up more than 40 percent of Pakistan's population, is a harsh one (i.e., a military government). It is no wonder, then, that the parliamentary system Pakistan inherited from its days of British rule broke down within four years of independence, which was gained in 1947 when Great Britain split British India into Muslim-majority Pakistan and Hindu-majority India. After the 1948 death of Pakistan's founder, Mohammad Ali Jinnah, British-trained civilian bureaucrats ran the country with the help of the army until 1958, when the army booted out the bureaucrats and took over. Since then there have been four military coups, and the army has ruled the country for 33 of its 61 years in existence.

While Pakistani politics is rarely if ever discussed in this context, the country's military leadership implicitly understands the dilemma of holding onto the buffer regions to the north and west. Long before military leader Gen. Mohammed Zia-ul-Haq (1977-1988) began Islamizing the state, the army's central command sought to counter the secular, left-wing, ethno-nationalist tendencies of the minority provinces by promoting an Islamic identity, particularly in the Pashtun belt. At first, the idea was to strengthen the religious underpinning of the republic in order to meld the outlands more closely with the core. Later, in the wake of the Soviet military intervention in Afghanistan (1978-1989), Pakistan's army began using radical Islamism as an arm of foreign policy. Islamist militant groups, trained or otherwise aided by the government, were formed to push Islamabad's influence into both Afghanistan and Indian-administered Kashmir.

As Pakistan would eventually realize, however, the strategy of promoting an Islamic identity to maintain domestic cohesion while using radical Islamism as an instrument of foreign policy would do far more harm than good.

Militant Proxies

Pakistan's Islamization policy culminated in the 1980s, when Pakistani, U.S. and Saudi intelligence services collaborated to drive Soviet troops out of Afghanistan by arming, funding and training mostly Pashtun Afghan fighters. When the Soviets withdrew in

1989, Pakistan was eager to forge a post-communist Islamist republic in Afghanistan — one that would be loyal to Islamabad and hostile to New Delhi. To that end, Pakistan's Inter-Services Intelligence (ISI) agency threw most of its support behind Islamist rebel leader Gulbuddin Hekmatyar of Hizb-i-Islami.

But things did not quite go as planned. When the Marxist regime in Kabul finally fell in 1992, a major intra-Islamist power struggle ensued, and Hekmatyar lost much of his influence. Amid the chaos, a small group of madrassa teachers and students who had fought against the Soviets rose above the factions and consolidated control over Afghanistan's Kandahar region in 1994. The ISI became so impressed by this Taliban movement that it dropped Hekmatyar and joined with the Saudis in ensuring that the Taliban would emerge as the vanguard of the Pashtuns and the rulers of Kabul.

The ISI was not the only one competing for the Taliban's attention. A small group of Arabs led by Osama bin Laden reopened shop in Afghanistan in 1996, looking to use a Taliban-run government in Afghanistan as a launch pad for reviving the caliphate. Ultimately, this would involve overthrowing all secular governments in the Muslim world (including the one sitting in Islamabad.) The secular, military-run government in Pakistan, on the other hand, was looking to use its influence on the Taliban government to wrest control of Kashmir from India. While Pakistan's ISI occasionally collaborated with al Qaeda in Afghanistan on matters of convenience, its goals were still ultimately incompatible with those of bin Laden. Pakistan was growing weary of al Qaeda's presence on its western border but soon became preoccupied with an opportunity developing to the east.

The Pakistani military saw an indigenous Muslim uprising in Indian-administered Kashmir in 1989 as a way to revive its claims over Muslim-majority Kashmir. It did not take long before the military began developing small guerrilla armies of Kashmiri Islamist irregulars for operations against India. When he was a two-star general and the army's director-general of military operations, former Pakistani President Pervez Musharraf played a leading role in refining the plan, which became fully operational in the 1999 Kargil War.

Pakistan's war strategy was to infiltrate Kashmiri Islamist guerrillas across the Line of Control (LoC) while Pakistani forces occupied high-altitude positions on Kargil Mountain. When India became aware of the infiltration, it sought to dislodge the guerrillas, at which point Pakistani artillery opened up on Indian troops positioned at lower-altitude base camps. While the Pakistani plan was initially successful, Indian forces soon regained the upper hand and U.S. pressure helped force a Pakistani retreat.

But the defeat at Kargil did not stop Pakistan from pursuing its Islamist militant proxy project in Kashmir. Groups such as Lashkar-e-Taiba (LeT), Hizb-ul-Mujahideen, Harkat-ul-Jihad-al-Islami, Jaish-e-Mohammed (JeM) and Al Badr spread their offices and training camps throughout Pakistani-occupied Kashmir under the guidance of the ISI. Whenever Islamabad felt compelled to turn up the heat on New Delhi, these militants would carry out operations against Indian targets, mostly in the Kashmir region.

India, meanwhile, would return the pressure on Islamabad by supporting Balochi rebels in western Pakistan and providing covert support to the ethnic Tajik-dominated Northern Alliance, the Taliban's main rival in Afghanistan. While Pakistan grew more and more distracted by supporting its Islamist proxies in Kashmir, the Taliban grew more attached to al Qaeda, which provided fighters to help the Taliban against the Northern Alliance as well as funding when the Taliban were crippled by an international embargo. As a result, al Qaeda extended its influence over the Taliban government, which gave al Qaeda free rein to plan and stage the deadliest terrorist attack to date against the West.

The Post 9/11 Environment

On Sept. 11, 2001, when the World Trade Center towers and the Pentagon were attacked, the United States put Pakistan in a chokehold: cooperate immediately in toppling the Taliban regime, which Pakistan had nurtured for years, or face destruction. Musharraf tried to buy some time by reaching out to Taliban leaders like Mullah

Omar to give up bin Laden, but the Taliban chief refused, making it clear that Pakistan had lost against al Qaeda in the battle for influence over the Taliban.

Just a few months after the 9/11 attacks, in December 2001, Kashmiri Islamist militants launched a major attack on the Indian parliament in New Delhi. Still reeling from the pressure it was receiving from the United States, Islamabad was now faced with the wrath of India. Both dealing with an Islamist militant threat, New Delhi and Washington tag-teamed Islamabad and tried to get it to cut its losses and dismantle its Islamist militant proxies.

To fend off some of the pressure, the Musharraf government banned LeT and JeM, two key Kashmiri Islamist groups fostered by the ISI and with close ties to al Qaeda. India was unsatisfied with the ban, which was mostly for show, and proceeded to mass a large military force along the LoC in Kashmir. The Pakistanis responded with their own deployment, and the two countries stood at the brink of nuclear war. U.S. intervention allowed India and Pakistan to step back from the precipice. In the process, Washington extracted concessions from Islamabad on the counterterrorism front, and official Pakistani support for the Afghan Taliban withered within days.

The Devolution of the ISI

The post 9/11 shake-up ignited a major crisis in the Pakistani military establishment. On one hand, the military was under extreme pressure to stamp out the jihadists along its western border. On the other hand, the military was fearful of U.S. and Indian interests aligning against Pakistan. Islamabad's primary means of keeping Washington as an ally was its connection to the jihadist insurgency in Afghanistan. So Islamabad played a double game, offering piecemeal cooperation to the United States while maintaining ties with its Islamist militant proxies in Afghanistan.

But the ISI's grip over these proxies was already loosening. In the run-up to 9/11, al Qaeda not only had close ties to the Taliban regime but also had reached out to ISI handlers whose job it was to maintain links with the array of Islamist militant proxies supported by Islamabad. Many of the intelligence operatives who had embraced the Islamist ideology were working to sabotage Islamabad's new alliance with Washington, which threatened to destroy the Islamist militant universe they had created. While the ISI leadership was busy trying to adjust to the post-9/11 operating environment, others within the middle and junior ranks of the agency started to engage in activities not necessarily sanctioned by their leadership.

As the influence of the Pakistani state declined, al Qaeda's influence rose. By the end of 2003, Musharraf had become the target of at least three al Qaeda assassination attempts. In the spring of 2004, Musharraf — again under pressure from the United States — was forced to send troops into the tribal badlands for the first time in the history of the country. Pakistani military operations to root out foreign fighters ended up killing thousands in the Pashtun areas and creating massive resentment against the central government.

In October 2006, when a deadly U.S. Predator strike hit a madrassah in Bajaur agency, killing 82 people, the stage was set for a jihadist insurgency to move into Pakistan proper. The Pakistani Taliban linked up with al Qaeda to carry out scores of suicide attacks, most against military targets and all aiming to break Islamabad's resolve to combat the insurgency. A major political debacle threw Islamabad off course in March 2007, when Musharraf's government was hit by a pro-democracy movement after he dismissed the country's chief justice. Four months later, a raid on Islamabad's Red Mosque, which Islamist militants had occupied, threw more fuel onto the insurgent fires, igniting suicide attacks in major Pakistani cities like Karachi and Islamabad, while the writ of the state continued to erode in the NWFP and FATA.

Musharraf was forced to step down as army chief in November 2007 and as president in August 2008, ushering in an incoherent civilian government. In December 2007, the world got a good glimpse of just how dangerous the murky ISI-jihadist nexus had become when the political chaos in Islamabad was exploited with a bold suicide attack that killed Pakistani opposition leader Benazir

136

Bhutto. Historically, the Pakistani military had been relied on to step in and restore order in such a crisis, but the military itself was coming undone as the split widened between those willing and those unwilling to work with the jihadists. Now, in the final days of 2008, the jihadist insurgency is raging on both sides of the Afghan-Pakistani border, with the country's only guarantor against collapse — the military — in disarray.

Kashmiri Groups Cut Loose

India has watched warily as Pakistan's jihadist problems have intensified over the past several years. Of utmost concern to New Delhi have been the scores of Kashmiri Islamist militants who had been operating on the ISI's payroll — and who had a score to settle with India. As Pakistan became more and more distracted with battling jihadists within its own borders, the Kashmiri Islamist militant groups began loosening their bonds with the Pakistani state. Groups such as LeT and JeM, who had been banned and forced underground following the 2001 Indian Parliament attack, started spreading their tentacles into major Indian cities. These groups retained links to the ISI, but the Pakistani military had bigger issues to deal with and needed to distance itself from the Kashmiri Islamists. If these groups were to continue to carry out operations, Pakistan needed some plausible deniability.

Over the past several years, Kashmiri Islamist militant groups have carried out sporadic attacks throughout India. The attacks have involved commercial-grade explosives rather than the military-grade RDX that is traditionally used in Pakistani-sponsored attacks, another sign that the groups are distancing themselves from Pakistan. The attacks, mostly against crowded transportation hubs, religious sites (both Hindu and Muslim) and marketplaces, have been designed to ignite riots between Hindus and Muslims that would compel the Indian government to crack down and revive the Kashmir cause.

However, India's Hindu nationalist and largely moderate Muslim communities failed to take the bait. It was only a matter of time before these militant groups began seeking out more strategic targets that would affect India's economic lifelines and ignite a crisis between India and Pakistan. As these groups became increasingly autonomous, they also started linking up with members of al Qaeda's transnational jihadist movement, who had a keen interest in stirring up conflict between India and Pakistan to divert the attention of Pakistani forces to the east.

By November 2008, this confluence of forces — Pakistan's raging jihadist insurgency, the devolution of the ISI and the increasing autonomy of the Kashmiri groups — created the conditions for one of the largest militant attacks in history to hit Mumbai, highlighting the extent to which Pakistan has lost control over its Islamist militant proxies.

Islamabad's Place in Washington's Strategy
March 27, 2009

U.S. President Barack Obama outlined his administration's strategy for the Afghan war in a March 27 press conference. Among the strategy's elements are more trainers for the Afghan military, more troops to hunt the Taliban and al Qaeda, and deeper integration between U.S. troops and their Afghan counterparts.

The part of the plan that most caught STRATFOR's attention was the sharp change in the tone of the rhetoric used toward Pakistan and the strategy's inclusion of $1.5 billion in assistance to Pakistan's civilian government annually for five years (subject to certain conditions, of course). This amount is more or less what the Bush administration spent on the Musharraf regime.

This adjustment in tone and funding marks a fairly sharp shift in recent U.S. policy toward Pakistan, and hints at a change in the overall focus of American foreign policy away from Afghanistan and toward Russia. But before understanding where U.S. policy is going, it is important to examine where it has been.

Until late 2008, the effectiveness of U.S. policy in Afghanistan was largely restricted because of power groups deeply enmeshed within the United States' primary "ally" in the Afghan war: Pakistan. Pakistan has always been militarily inferior to its primary rival, India, and so has had to foster various militant Islamist groups in order to counter India's conventional military strength. These groups also proved essential both in Pakistan's opposition to the Soviet occupation of Afghanistan during the Cold War and in maintaining Pakistani influence both before and after the Sept. 11, 2001, attacks.

Herein lies the rub. In October 2001, the Americans essentially forced the Pakistanis to facilitate the American hunt for al Qaeda in Afghanistan. This resulted in many of the militant Islamists who are so critical to Pakistani foreign policy feeling betrayed. This in turn led them to either turn on their masters or ally with elements within the Pakistani military and intelligence establishments to oppose American — and by extension, Pakistani — military policy in Afghanistan. Most of these militants were not Kashmiri or even Afghan, but actually from Pakistan's northwestern regions. In essence, the American pursuit of al Qaeda in Afghanistan triggered a Pakistani civil war.

It is a war that the Pakistani government has not been particularly enthusiastic about fighting. Not only are most of the belligerents actual Pakistanis who retain deep links into the Pakistani military establishment, but many Pakistani policymakers see the militants as the most effective foreign policy tool Pakistan has ever had. Even those willing to hunt down their own have faced constant obstacles from those who disagree, which certainly saps the war effort. The result is that Pakistan is — at best — an unwilling participant in U.S. military operations, and lackluster Pakistani assistance has lessened American effectiveness in Afghanistan. This has also resulted in massive security complications for NATO convoys that are forced to transit Pakistan en route to the war in Afghanistan. Yet because Pakistan was critical to the war effort, there was little the Americans could do except bribe the Pakistanis to do more, a policy that — especially when one considers what the stakes are in a civil war — has met with understandably thin results.

The Mumbai attacks of November 2008 — in which some of these Pakistani-linked militants killed several hundred people in India — raised the possibility of a new strategy. The trick was to make Islamabad feel that it had no options but to more aggressively prosecute the war. This would require leveraging Indian anger to scare the Pakistanis on one hand and forging an alternative supply route through Central Asia so that NATO would not depend so much on the Pakistanis on the other. Pakistan would be isolated, and would face the choice of cooperating more thoroughly or risk cracking apart under the strain of a civil war the United States no longer had a stake in. It was the ultimate bad-cop strategy.

With Obama's announcement to grant $1.5 billion in annual aid — slightly more than 1 percent of Pakistan's gross domestic product — for five years, the Obama administration appears to be emphasizing the good-cop strategy over the bad-cop one and switching back to attempts to influence Pakistan via positive incentives.

The Obama announcement, therefore, raises three questions:

- Why go back to playing good cop? Critics may charge that the new Obama plan is simply reverting to the Bush administration strategy, which has not done particularly well at "winning" the Afghan war. But there are two reasons the bad-cop strategy was always a shot in the dark. First, for the bad-cop strategy to work, the United States cannot be dependent upon Pakistan. It would require a robust supply line to Afghanistan that transits the Russian sphere of influence in Central Asia. In addition to the logistical difficulties of this alternative route to ferry supplies from the north, the Russians' price for such a supply route is for the United States not just to abandon its ambitions for Central Asia but to forge a new continental security relationship that would roll back much of the economic, political and military gains the United States has made since the end of the Cold War. The Obama administration seems to have come to the conclusion that getting a leg up in the Afghan war is not worth the reforging of the Soviet Union. Furthermore, even if the plan were perfectly executed and the Russians blamelessly cooperative, forcing Pakistan to act against its basic self interest would have led to sporadic cooperation from the Pakistanis at best. No matter what plan was used, Pakistan would still border Afghanistan, and the border region would still be critical to the war effort. U.S. forces were going to continue to pursue militants on both sides of the border, and that meant U.S. forces would regularly violate Pakistani sovereignty. Pakistan simply cannot be cut out of the process because it is a significant part of the problem. Put differently, the routes through Moscow's sphere of influence are not an alternative to the ones from Pakistan, though there is likely to be limited cooperation with Moscow and the Central Asian states for one or more supplementary routes.

- To what degree can the Pakistanis supply any assistance? Considering the depth of Pakistani opposition to U.S. policies, and the fact that the more recalcitrant members of Pakistan's military and intelligence establishments will see the Obama plan as a reason to continue resistance, in all practicality the best that can be hoped for is that Pakistan will supply more security to NATO convoys. Anything more is simply wishful thinking.

- What is necessary to make the new strategy work? The answer to this one is simple: troops, and lots of them. With Pakistan providing at best limited support, Obama is going to be utterly reliant upon the Europeans to provide more manpower. Which is why the announcement came on Friday, March 27; next week, Obama will be in Europe for the G20 summit and the NATO summit. These are the venues at which Obama will make his case for assistance.

Conceptually, the Obama plan is about as sound as a plan for Afghanistan can be, but then again, so was the Bush plan — which the Obama plan is essentially continuing. And as Bush discovered, "conceptually sound" and "operationally sound" are two very different things.

The Fault Line Between National and Transnational Ambitions
April 5, 2009

The United States is in the process of trying to reach out to reconcilable elements among the Taliban movement, as part of its efforts to try and bring an end to the insurgency in Afghanistan. However, Washington does not possess a reliable map of the Taliban landscape, which is critical to identifying pragmatic factions. Further complicating this problem is a huge trust deficit between the Obama administration and Pakistan, the only player that could assist the Americans in this task, given Islamabad's historical role as the principal state actor that aided the rise of the Taliban movement.

But the Pakistanis are struggling with their own jihadist problem, forced to fight the "bad" Taliban (those who are waging war against Pakistan) while trying to retain influence over the "good" ones (those who are focused on the fighting in Afghanistan). From Pakistan's point of view, the only way it can contain the insurgency within its own borders is by working with those elements that do not stage attacks in Pakistan and/or remain within the Pakistani sphere of influence against the renegades. This approach is quite similar to what Saudi Arabia did to contain its insurgency in 2003-2004: redirect the jihadists' attention away from the kingdom to Iraq.

In particular, the Pakistanis rely on the Haqqani network, which reportedly has also been in talks with the Afghan government, in order to fight the Tehrik-i-Taliban Pakistan (TTP), Pakistan's largest

Taliban grouping and a faction responsible for a wave of attacks all across the country. In fact, the de facto leader of the Haqqani network, Sirajuddin Haqqani, has reportedly been involved in efforts to mediate between Pakistani authorities and TTP chief Baitullah Mehsud. Haqqani and Mehsud represent a key divide in the cross-border Taliban landscape, with the former wanting to focus militant activity in Afghanistan and the latter in favor of expanding the jihadist war into Pakistan.

This fault line between national and transnational ambitions is a potential starting point for the process of collapsing the insurgency from within. In fact, the Obama administration has begun to make the distinction between the Taliban and al Qaeda. But driving a wedge between al Qaeda and the Taliban requires separating Taliban elements that are prepared to part ways with the transnational jihadist network from those who are not.

The Afghan Taliban see their mandate as Afghanistan, while al Qaeda seeks to create a transnational "Islamic" polity. Obviously, these are not neat categories. There are Taliban forces that are aligned with al Qaeda's objective, and prime examples are Pakistani Taliban groups such as Mehsud's TTP and Punjabi/Kashmiri groups such as Lashkar-e-Jhangvi, Lashkar-e-Taiba and Jaish-e-Mohammed. The Pashtun jihadists and their Punjab-based allies are intensifying their war against Islamabad, raising fears of the Taliban taking over inside Pakistan.

Because Islamabad lacks financial and military tools and political will, it is losing ground to its own Taliban rebels. Therefore, financial aid from and military cooperation with the United States will not work without the two agreeing upon the distinction between the "good" and "bad" Taliban and coordinating negotiations with the insurgents, which is what is needed to rein in the escalating militancy.

Such an arrangement is likely because, despite their disagreements regarding Afghanistan, Washington and Islamabad agree on the need to prevent the Talibanization of Pakistan. The two also agree that success in the Afghan war will require the incorporation of at least some elements of the Taliban into a future Afghan power structure as a means to end the insurgency — much like the approach that worked so well with Sunni insurgents in Iraq.

Even though the United States recently unveiled a new Afghan strategy, which entails greater cooperation with Pakistan and an emphasis on a negotiated settlement with pragmatic Afghan Taliban, Washington simply is not very far along in understanding the various factional breakdowns within the Taliban. To a certain degree, this is quite understandable given the opaque nature of the cross-border Taliban phenomenon and the complexity of the relations the Pashtun jihadists have with al Qaeda and with elements of the Pakistani security establishment. This is the reason the Americans have increased pressure on Islamabad to aggressively crack down on jihadists and have launched unmanned aerial vehicle strikes in the tribal badlands.

The Pakistanis, however, possess an in-depth understanding of the Taliban — something that comes from years of extensive collaboration resulting from the simple fact that Pakistan's Inter-Services Intelligence directorate helped create the Taliban in the first place and is also more aware of the current jihadist reality in its own territory, especially the Pashtun northwest.

Yet the Americans have been bitter about the Pakistanis' selective approach to the militants. From the U.S. viewpoint, while there is the theoretical benefit of differentiation, Pakistan's differentiation directly encourages attacks in Afghanistan. As far as Washington has been concerned, there is no distinction between those who are fighting U.S./NATO/Afghan forces in Afghanistan and those who are battling the Pakistani state. This would explain why Washington last week announced bounties on the heads of both Mehsud and Haqqani, since both have ties to the al Qaeda network.

The Reality of Risk in Pakistan
April 27, 2009

Pakistan is the primary channel through which U.S. and NATO supplies travel to support the war effort in Afghanistan. The reason for this is quite simple: Pakistan offers the shortest and most logistically viable overland supply routes for Western forces operating in landlocked Afghanistan. Once Pakistan found itself in the throes of an intensifying insurgency mid-2007, however, U.S. military strategists had to seriously consider whether the United States would be able to rely on Pakistan to keep these supply lines open, especially when military plans called for increasing the number of troops in theater.

In late 2008, as Pakistan continued its downward spiral, U.S. Central Command (CENTCOM) chief Gen. David Petraeus began touring Central Asian capitals in an attempt to stitch together supplemental supply lines into northern Afghanistan. Soon enough, Washington learned that it was fighting an uphill battle trying to negotiate in Russian-dominated Central Asia without first reaching a broader understanding with Moscow. With U.S.-Russian negotiations now in flux and the so-called "northern distribution network" frozen, the United States has little choice but to face the reality in Pakistan.

This reality is rooted in the Pakistani Taliban's desire to spread south beyond the Pashtun-dominated northwest tribal badlands (where attacks against the U.S./NATO supply lines are already intensifying) into the Pakistani core in Punjab province. Punjab is Pakistan's industrial heartland and home to more than half of the entire Pakistani population. If the Taliban manage to establish a foothold in Punjab, then the idea of a collapsing Pakistani state would actually become a realistic scenario. The key to preventing such a scenario is keeping the Pakistani military, the country's most powerful institution, intact. However, splits within the military over how to handle the insurgency while preserving ties with militant proxies are threatening the military's cohesion. Moreover, the threats to the supply lines go even further south than Punjab. The port of Karachi in Sindh province, where U.S./NATO supplies are offloaded from ships, could be destabilized if the Taliban provoke local political forces.

In league with their jihadist brethren across the border in Afghanistan, the Pakistani Taliban and their local affiliates are just as busy planning their next steps in the insurgency as the United States is in planning its counterinsurgency strategy. Afghanistan is a country that is not kind to outsiders, and the overwhelming opinion of the jihadist forces battling Western, Pakistani and Afghan troops in the region is that this is a war that can be won through the power of exhaustion. Key to this strategy will be an attempt to make the position of U.S. and NATO forces in Afghanistan untenable by increasing risk to their supply lines in Pakistan.

A Dearth of Security Options

As the pre-eminent global maritime power, the United States is able to sustain military operations far beyond its coastlines. Afghanistan, however, is a landlocked country whose inaccessibility prevents the U.S. military from utilizing its naval prowess. Instead, the United States and NATO must bring in troops, munitions and militarily sensitive materiel directly by air and rely on long, overland supply routes through Pakistan for non-lethal supplies such as food, building materials and fuel (most of which is refined in Pakistan). This logistical challenge is compounded by the fact that the overland supply routes run through a country that is trying to battle its own jihadist insurgency.

The deteriorating security situation in Pakistan now requires an effective force to protect the supply convoys. Though sending a couple of U.S./NATO brigades into Pakistan would provide first-rate security for these convoys, such an option would be political dynamite in U.S.-Pakistani relations. Pakistan already has an extremely low tolerance for CIA activity and U.S. unmanned aerial vehicle attacks on its soil. The sight of Western forces operating openly in the country

LOGISTICS AND AFGHANISTAN

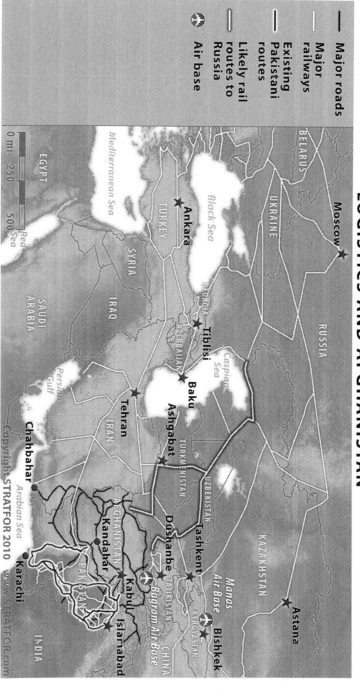

Legend:
- Major roads
- Major railways
- Existing Pakistani routes
- Likely rail routes to Russia
- ✈ Air base

would be a red line that Islamabad simply could not cross. Even if this were an option, U.S./NATO forces are already stretched to the limit in Afghanistan and there are no troops to spare to send into Pakistan — nor is there the desire on the part of the United States or NATO to insert their troops into such a dicey security situation.

Enlisting the Pakistani military would be another option, but the Pentagon has thus far resisted allowing the Pakistani military to take direct charge of protecting and transporting U.S./NATO supplies through Pakistan into Afghanistan. The reasons for this are unclear, but they likely can be attributed (at least in part) to U.S. distrust for the Pakistani military-intelligence apparatus, which is heavily infiltrated by Islamist sympathizers who retain links to their militant Islamist proxies.

Instead, CENTCOM's logistics team has given the security responsibility to private Pakistani security contractors. This has not been unusual in recent U.S. military campaigns, which have come to rely on private contractors for many logistical and security functions, including local firms in countries linked to the military supply chain. In Pakistan, such contractors provide security escorts to Pakistani truck drivers who transport supplies from the port of Karachi through Pakistan via a northern route and a southern route into Afghanistan, where the supplies are then delivered to key logistical hubs. While this approach provided sufficient security in the early years of the Afghan campaign, it has recently become an issue because of increasingly aggressive attacks by Taliban and other militants in Pakistan.

STRATFOR is told that many within the Pakistani military have long resented the fact that Washington has not entrusted them with the responsibility to secure the routes. The reasons behind the Pakistani military's complaints are twofold. First, the military feels that its authority is being undermined by the dealings between the U.S. military and local contractors. Even beyond these deals, the Pakistani military consistently expresses its frustration when it is not the chief interlocutor with the United States in Pakistan, and has done so when U.S. officials have met with local leaders in the country and with the civilian government in Islamabad.

THREAT ASSESSMENT: U.S./NATO SUPPLY LINES IN PAKISTAN

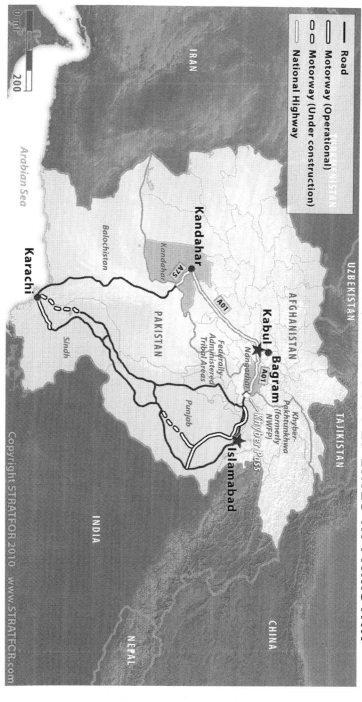

	Road
	Motorway (Operational)
	Motorway (Under construction)
	National Highway

0 mi²⁰⁰

Second, there is a deep financial interest on the part of the Pakistani military, which does not want to miss out on the large profits reaped by private security contractors in protecting the supply routes. As a result, Pakistani security forces are believed to turn a blind eye and occasionally even facilitate attacks on U.S. and NATO convoys in Pakistan in order to pressure Washington into giving the contracts to the better-equipped Pakistani military. That said, it is unclear whether the Pakistani military could fulfill such a commitment since the military itself is already stretched thin between its operations along the Afghan-Pakistani border and its massive military focus on the eastern border with India.

Many of the private Pakistani security companies guarding the routes are owned by wealthy Pakistani civilians who have strong links to the government and to retired military officials. The private Pakistani security firms currently guarding the routes include Ghazi Security, Ready Guard, Phoenix Security Agency and SE Security Agency. Most of the main offices of these companies are located in Islamabad, but these contractors have also hired smaller security agencies in Peshawar. The private companies that own terminals used for the northern and southern supply routes include al Faisal Terminal (whose owner has been kidnapped by militants and his whereabouts are unknown); Bilal Terminal (owned by Shahid Ansari from Punjab); World Port Logistics (owned by Major Fakhar, a nephew of former Pakistani President Gen. Pervez Musharraf); Raziq International; Peace Line; Pak-Afghan; and Waqar Terminal.

While the owners of these security firms make a handsome profit from the U.S./NATO military contracts, the guards who actually drive and protect the trucks ferrying supplies make a meager salary, somewhere between 4,000 and 5,000 rupees (under $65) per month. Not surprisingly, the security is shoddy, with three to five poorly trained and equipped guards usually spread throughout a convoy who are easily overrun by Taliban forces that frequently attack the convoys in hordes. Given their poor compensation, these security guards feel little compulsion to hold their positions and resist concerted assaults.

The motivations for attacks against the supply infrastructure can vary. The Taliban and their jihadist affiliates are ideologically driven to target Western forces and increase the cost for them to remain in the region. There are also a number of criminally motivated fighters who adopt the Taliban label as a convenient cover but who are far more interested in making a profit. Both groups can benefit from racketeering enterprises that allow them to extort hefty protection fees from private security firms in return for the contractors' physical safety.

One Pakistani truck driver relayed a story in which he was told by a suspected Taliban operative to leave his truck and come back in the morning to drive to Afghanistan. When the driver returned he found the truck on fire. Inadequate security allows for easy infiltration and manipulation by Pakistan's Inter-Services Intelligence agency, which is already heavily penetrated by Islamist sympathizers. Drivers will often strike a deal with the militants allowing raids on the convoys in return for a cut of the proceeds once the goods are sold on the black market. One indication of just how porous U.S./NATO security arrangements are in Pakistan is that the commander of the most active Taliban faction in Khyber agency, Mangal Bagh of Lashkar-e-Islami (LI), is allegedly a former transporter himself now using jihad as a cover for his criminal activities.

STRATFOR is not aware of any plans by the Pentagon to turn these security contracts over to the Pakistani military. It is even more unclear whether doing so would do much to improve the situation. If the U.S. military continues to rely on these contractors to guard the supply routes in the face of a growing Taliban threat, certain changes could be made to enhance the contractors' capabilities. Already, U.S. logistics teams are revising the northern route by moving some of the supply depots farther south in Punjab where the security threat is lower (though the Taliban are attempting to expand their presence there). More funding could also be directed toward these security contractors to ensure that the guards protecting the convoys are properly trained and sufficiently paid to give them more of an incentive to resist Taliban attacks. Nonetheless, the current outsourcing to private

Pakistani security firms is evidently fraught with complications that are unlikely to be resolved in the near term.

Karachi: The Starting Point

Both supply routes originate in Pakistan's largest city and primary seaport, Karachi. The city is Pakistan's financial hub and provides critical ocean access for U.S./NATO logistics support in Afghanistan. If Karachi — a city already known to have a high incidence of violence — were to destabilize, the Western military supply chain could be threatened even before supplies embarked on the lengthy and volatile journey through the rest of Pakistan.

There are two inter-linking security risks in Karachi: the local ruling party — the Mutahiddah Qaumi Movement (MQM) — and the Islamist militancy. The MQM is a political movement representing the Muhajir ethnic community of Muslims who migrated to Pakistan from India. Since its rise in the 1980s, the party has demonstrated a proclivity for ethnic-driven violence through its armed cadres. While the MQM does not have a formal militia and is part of the Sindh provincial legislature as well as the national parliament, the party is very sensitive about any challenges to its power base in the metropolitan Karachi area and controls powerful organized crime groups in the city. On many occasions, clashes between MQM and other rival political forces have paralyzed the city.

Ideologically speaking, the MQM is secular and has been firmly opposed to Islamist groups since its inception. The party has been watching nervously as the Taliban have crept southward from their stronghold in the country's northwest. In recent weeks, the MQM also has been the loudest political voice in the country sounding the alarm against the growing jihadist threat. The party is well aware that any jihadist strategy that aims to strike at Pakistan's economic nerve center and the most critical node of the U.S./NATO supply lines makes Karachi a prime target.

The MQM is particularly concerned that Baitullah Mehsud's Tehrik-i-Taliban Pakistan (TTP) will try to encroach on its turf in

Karachi. While the Waziristan-based TTP itself has very little presence in Karachi, it does have a jihadist network in the city that could be utilized. Many Taliban members come from Pashtun tribes and derive much of their political support from Pashtun populations. Karachi has a Pashtun population of 3.5 million, making up some 30 percent of the city's population. Moreover, Karachi police have reported that Taliban members are among the "several hundred thousand" tribesmen fleeing violence in the frontier regions who have settled on the outskirts of Karachi.

Jihadists have thus far demonstrated a limited ability to operate in the city. In 2002, jihadists kidnapped and killed U.S. journalist Daniel Pearl and attacked the U.S. Consulate. In a 2007 suicide attack on a vehicle belonging to the U.S. Consulate in Karachi, jihadists killed a U.S. diplomat and injured 52 others on the eve of one of then-President George W. Bush's rare trips to Pakistan. A host of Pakistani jihadist groups as well as "al Qaeda Prime" (its core leadership) have been active in the area, evidenced by the capture of Ramzi bin al-Shibh, deputy coordinator of the 9/11 attacks, in Karachi in 2002.

Until now the MQM did not perceive the Taliban to be a direct threat to its hold over the city, but the MQM is now feeling vulnerable given the Taliban's spread in the north. There has been a historic tension between the MQM and the significant Pashtun minority in Karachi. The MQM regards this minority with deep suspicion because it believes the Pashtuns could provide a safe haven for Pashtun jihadists seeking to extend their influence to the south.

In the wake of the "Shariah for peace" agreement in the Swat district of Pakistan's North-West Frontier Province (NWFP), tensions have risen between the MQM and the country's largest Pashtun political group, the Awami National Party (ANP), which rules the NWFP and is the party chiefly responsible for negotiating the peace agreement with the Tehrik-Nifaz-i-Shariat-i-Muhammadi (TNSM), the jihadist group in the greater Swat region. MQM's 19 members of parliament were the only ones who did not vote in favor of the Swat peace deal, which has amplified its concerns over the threat of Talibanization in Pakistan. In response, TNSM leader Maulana Sufi

Muhammad has declared parliamentarians who oppose the Nizam-i-Adl Regulation non-Muslims. The MQM is also trying to mobilize religious groups that oppose the Sunni Islamic Deobandi movement, particularly Barelvis, against the Taliban.

With rising Muhajir-Pashtun ethnic tensions, the MQM-ANP spat and the MQM's fear of a jihadist threat to its authority, conditions in Karachi are slowly building toward a confrontation. Should jihadists demonstrate a capability to step up operations in the city, the MQM will show little to no restraint in cracking down on the city's Pashtun minority through its armed cadres, which would lead to wider-scale clashes between the MQM and the Pashtun community. There is a precedent for urban conflict in Karachi, and it could cause authorities to impose a citywide curfew that would disrupt operations at the port and impede supplies from making their way out of the city.

The situation described above is still a worst-case scenario. Since Karachi is the financial center of the country, the MQM-controlled local government, the federal government in Islamabad and the Rawalpindi-based military establishment all share an interest in preserving stability in this key city. It will also likely take some time before Pakistani jihadists are able to project power that far south. Even a few days or weeks of turmoil in Karachi, however, will threaten the country's economy — which is already on the verge of bankruptcy — and further undercut the weakened state's ability to address the growing insecurity. So far, the MQM has kept its hold over Karachi, but the Taliban already have their eyes on the city, and it would not take much to provoke the MQM into a confrontation that could threaten a crucial link in the U.S./NATO supply chain.

The Northern Route

The northern route through Pakistan, used for transporting the bulk of U.S./NATO overland supplies to Afghanistan, travels through four provinces — Sindh, Punjab, the NWFP and the tribal badlands of the Federally Administered Tribal Areas (FATA) — before it snakes its way through the Khyber Pass to reach the Torkham border crossing with Afghanistan.

Convoys generally travel on main north-south national highway N-5 or a combination of N-5 and N-55 from Karachi to Torkham, a distance that can range from approximately 1,325 kilometers to 1,820 kilometers. Most transporters say they prefer the combination of N-5 and N-55, which allows them to cut across Sindh by switching from N-5 to N-65 near Sukkur and then jumping onto N-55 at Shikarpur before heading into Punjab. A small percentage of trucks (some 5 percent) use a combination of national highways and what are called "motorways," essentially expressways that allow for better security, have no traffic lights and avoid urban centers. These motorways also have fewer chokepoints and thus fewer opportunities for militant ambushes, but they also lack rest stops, which is why most convoys travel on the national highways.

Pakistani transporters tell STRATFOR that they typically decide on a day-to-day basis whether to go the longer N-5 route or the shorter N-55 route. If they feel the security situation is bad enough, they are far more likely to take the longer N-5 route to Peshawar, which reduces their risk because it goes through less volatile areas — essentially, less of the NWFP. With the Taliban rapidly taking over territory in the NWFP, trucks are likely to rely more heavily on N-5.

Once the trucks leave Karachi, the stretch of road through Sindh province is the safest along the entire northern route. Most of Sindh, especially the rural areas, form the core support base of the secular Pakistan People's Party (PPP), which controls both the federal and the provincial governments. Outside of Karachi, there is virtually no serious militant Islamist presence in the province. However, small pockets of jihadists do pop up from time to time. In 2004, a top Pakistani militant leader, Amjad Farooqi of Jaish-e-Mohammed (JeM), who worked closely with al Qaeda Prime operational commander Abu Faraj al-Libi and was responsible for assassination attempts on Musharraf, was killed in a shootout with police in the town of Nawabshah in central Sindh.

Once out of Sindh and into Punjab province, the northern supply route enters the core of Pakistan, the political, industrial and agricultural heartland of the country where some 60 percent of the population is concentrated. The province is also the mainstay of the country's powerful military establishment, with six of the army's nine corps headquartered in the key urban areas of Rawalpindi, Mangla, Lahore, Gujranwala, Bahawalpur and Multan.

This province has not yet witnessed jihadist attacks targeting the U.S./NATO supply chain, but the jihadist threat in Punjab is slowly rising. Major jihadist figures have found a safe haven in the province, evidenced by the fact that several top al Qaeda leaders, including the mastermind of the 9/11 attacks, Khalid Sheikh Mohammed, were captured in various parts of Punjab, including Rawalpindi, Faisalabad and Gujarat. Punjab also has witnessed a number of high-profile jihadist attacks in major cities, including suicide bombings in the capital, Islamabad, and its twin city Rawalpindi (where the military is headquartered) as well as manpower-heavy armed assaults in the provincial capital, Lahore, where teams of gunmen have assaulted both moving and stationary targets. The attacks have mostly targeted Pakistani security installations and have been conducted mainly by Pashtun jihadists in conjunction with Punjabi jihadist allies. The bulk of jihadist activity in the province takes place in the northern part of Punjab, closer to the NWFP border, where suicide bombings have been concentrated.

The Punjabi jihadist phenomenon was born in the 1980s, when the military regime of Gen. Mohammed Zia-ul-Haq aggressively pursued a policy of Islamization to secure power and weaken his principal opponent, the PPP, whose government he had overthrown to come to power. It was during the Zia years that Pakistan, along with Saudi Arabia and the United States, was heavily involved in backing Islamist militias to fight the Marxist government and its allied Soviet troops in Afghanistan, where many of the Punjab-based groups joined the Pashtun groups and had their first taste of battle. Later in the 1990s, many of these Punjabi groups, who followed an extremist Deobandi interpretation of Sunni Islam, were used by the security establishment to support the rise of the Taliban in Afghanistan and to aid the insurgency in Indian-administered Kashmir. Sectarian groups like Sipah Sahaba Pakistan and Lashkar-e-Jhangvi (LeJ) were also developed to help the regime keep the Shiite minority in Pakistan contained.

Pakistan's Afghan and Kashmiri jihadist project suffered a major setback with the 9/11 attacks against the United States and the American response. Caught between contradictory objectives — the need to align itself with the United States and to preserve its Islamist militant assets — Pakistan eventually lost control of many of its former Islamist militant assets, who then started teaming up with al Qaeda-led transnational jihadists in the region.

Most alarming for Islamabad is the fact that these groups are now striking at the core of Pakistan in places like Lahore, where brazen assaults were launched on March 3 against a bus carrying the Sri Lankan national cricket team and on March 30 against a police academy. These attacks illustrated this trend of Pakistan's militant proxies turning against their erstwhile patron — first in the Pashtun areas and now in Punjab. The Lahore attacks both involved multi-man assault teams, a sign that the jihadists are able to use a large number of Islamist recruits from the province itself.

Though Pakistan came under massive pressure to crack down on these groups in the wake of the November 2008 Mumbai attacks in India, groups such as Lashkar-e-Taiba (LeT) have considerable influence in the Lahore region. Similarly, LeJ and JeM have growing pockets of support in various parts of Punjab, particularly in southern Seraiki-speaking districts such as Bahawalpur, Rahim Yar Khan and Dera Ghazi Khan. One of the major causes of rising support for such jihadist groups in Punjab was an incident in 2007, when a clerical family hailing from the border region between Punjab and Balochistan led an uprising at Islamabad's Red Mosque. The subsequent security operation to regain control of the mosque from the militants turned many locals against the military and sent them into the arms of the Islamists.

While the major urban areas of Punjab have not been spared by jihadists, most jihadist activity in the province is concentrated closer to the provincial border with the NWFP. The route that travels along N-5 must pass through Wah, Kamra and Attock, the three main towns of northwestern Punjab. Each of these towns has been rocked by suicide attacks. Attock was the scene of a July 2004 assassination attempt against former Prime Minister Shaukat Aziz. Kamra, home of the Pakistan Aeronautical Complex, an aircraft servicing and manufacturing facility, was the scene of a December 2007 suicide attack targeting a school bus carrying children of air force personnel. In August 2008 in Wah, a pair of suicide bombers struck Pakistan's main ordnance factory.

There are indications that such jihadist activity could creep farther south into the heart of Punjab and potentially target the U.S./NATO supply chain. The Taliban are growing bolder by the day now that they have made significant territorial gains in the greater Swat region in the NWFP farther north. As the security situation in the NWFP and FATA deteriorates, U.S./NATO supply depots and terminals are being moved further south to Punjab where they will be safer, or so it is thought. However, locals in the area are already protesting the relocation of these terminals because they know that they will run a greater chance of becoming Taliban targets the more closely attached they are to the U.S./NATO supply chain. These people have good reason to be nervous. The jihadists are now openly declaring grander intentions of spreading beyond the Pashtun-dominated periphery into Punjab, Pakistan's core. Though it would take some time to achieve this, these jihadist groups would have a strategic interest in carrying out attacks against Western supply lines in Punjab that could demonstrate the jihadist reach, aggravate already intense anti-U.S. sentiment and hamper U.S./NATO logistics for the war in Afghanistan.

The last leg of the northern supply line runs through the NWFP and the tribal badlands of the FATA. This is by far the most dangerous portion along the route and where Taliban activity is already reaching a crescendo.

Once in the NWFP the route goes through the district of Nowshera before it reaches the provincial capital Peshawar and begins to hug Taliban territory. A variety of Taliban groups based in the FATA, many of whom are part of the TTP umbrella organization and/or the Mujahideen Shura Council, have taken over several districts in western NWFP and are now on Peshawar's doorstep. There have been several attacks in Peshawar and further north in Charsadda, where former Interior Minister Aftab Ahmed Khan Sherpao twice escaped assassination at the hands of suicide bombers, and east in Nowshera, where an army base was targeted.

Though suicide attacks have occurred in these areas, the Pashtun jihadists are not in control of the territory in the NWFP that lies east of Peshawar. All attacks on the northern route have taken place to the west of Peshawar, on the stretch of N-5 between Peshawar and the Torkham border crossing, a distance of nearly 60 kilometers where jihadist activity is intensifying.

Once the transporters reach Peshawar, they hit what is called the "Ring Road" area, where 15 to 20 bus terminals are located for containers coming from Karachi to stop and then head toward Afghanistan through the Khyber Pass. The area where the bus terminals are situated is under the jurisdiction of Peshawar district, a settled and relatively calm area. But when the trucks travel east on the Peshawar-Torkham road toward Afghanistan, they enter a critical danger zone. Some Pakistani truckers have refused to drive this stretch between Peshawar and the Khyber Pass for fear of being attacked. Militants destroyed a key bridge in February on the Peshawar-Torkham road, where there are a dozen of other bridges that can be targeted in future attacks. The most recent and daring attack on highway N-5 between Peshawar and Torkham was the March 27 suicide bombing of a mosque during Friday prayers that killed dozens of local political and security officials.

For those convoys that make it out of the Peshawar terminal-depot hub, the next major stop is the Khyber Pass leading into Khyber agency, where the route travels along N-5 through Jamrud, Landikotal and Michni Post and then reaches the border with Afghanistan. The border area between Peshawar district and Khyber agency is called the Karkhano Market, which is essentially a massive black market for stolen goods run by smugglers, drug dealers and other organized-crime elements. Here one can find high quality merchandise at cheap prices, including stolen goods that were meant for U.S. and NATO forces. STRATFOR sources claim they have seen U.S./NATO military uniforms and laptops going for $100 in the market.

Khyber agency (the most developed agency in the tribal belt) has been the scene of high-profile abductions, destroyed bridges and attacks against local political and security officials. Considering the frequency of the attacks, it appears that the militants can strike at the supply chain with impunity, and with likely encouragement from Pakistani security forces. This area is inhabited by four tribes — the Afridi, Shinwari, Mullagori and Shimani. But as is the case in other agencies of the FATA, the mullahs and militia commanders have usurped the tribal elders in Khyber agency. As many as three different Taliban groups in this area are battling Pakistani forces as well as each other.

Militiamen of the most active Taliban faction in Khyber agency, Mangal Bagh's LI, heavily patrol the Bara area and have blown up several shrines, abducted local Christians and fought gunbattles with police. LI is not part of Baitullah Mehsud's TTP umbrella group but maintains significant influence among the tribal maliks. Mehsud is allied with another faction called the Hakimullah Group, which rivals a third faction called Amr bil Maarouf wa Nahi Anil Munkar ("Promotion of Virtue and Prevention of Vice"), whose leader, Haji Namdaar, was killed by Hakimullah militiamen.

Not all the Khyber agency militants are ideologically driven jihadists like Baitullah Mehsud of the TTP and Maulana Fazlullah of the TNSM. Some are organized-crime elements who lack religious training and have long been engaged in smuggling operations. When the Pakistani military entered the region to crack down on the insurgency, these criminal groups saw their illegal activities disrupted. To continue to earn a livelihood, many of these criminal elements were reborn as militants under the veil of jihad.

LI commander Bagh (the alleged former convoy driver) is uneducated overall, and never received any kind of formal religious education. He became the leader of LI two years ago when he succeeded Deobandi cleric Mufti Munir Shakir. Bagh stays clear of targeting Pakistani military forces and says his objective is to clean up the area's criminal elements and, like his counterparts in other parts of the Pashtun region, impose a Talibanesque interpretation of religious law. This tendency on the part of organized-crime elements in Pakistan to jump on the jihad bandwagon actually runs the risk of weakening the insurgency. Because criminal groups are not ideologically driven, it is easier for Pakistani forces and U.S. intelligence operatives to bribe them away from the insurgency.

The Southern Route

The southern route into Afghanistan is the shorter of the two U.S./NATO supply routes. The entire route traverses the 813-kilometer-long national highway N-25, running north from the port of Karachi through Sindh and northwest into Balochistan before crossing into southern Afghanistan at the Chaman border crossing.

About 25 to 30 percent of the supplies going to U.S./NATO forces operating in southern Afghanistan travel along this route. Though most of the southern route through Pakistan is relatively secure, the security risks rise dramatically once the trucks cross into Afghanistan on highway A-75, which runs through the heart of Taliban country in Kandahar province and surrounding areas.

Once out of Karachi, the route through Sindh is secure. Problems arise once the trucks hit Balochistan province, a resource-rich region where ethnic Baloch separatists have waged an insurgency for decades against Punjabi rule. The Baloch insurgency is directed against the Pakistani state and is led by three main groups: the Balochistan Liberation Army (BLA), the Balochistan Liberation Front (BLF) and the People's Liberation Army. The BLA is the most active of the three and focuses its attacks on Pakistani police and military personnel, natural gas pipelines and civil servants. The Pakistani military deals with the Baloch rebels with an iron fist, but the Baloch insurgency has been a long and insoluble one. (Balochistan enjoyed autonomy under the British, and when Pakistan was created it forcibly took over the province; successive Pakistani regimes have mishandled the issue.)

Once inside Balochistan, the supply route runs first into the major industrial town of Hub (also known as Hub Chowki) and then into the Baloch capital of Quetta. These are areas that have witnessed a number of Baloch separatist attacks in recent years, including the December 2004 bombing of a Pakistani military truck in Quetta (claimed by the BLA), the killing of three Chinese engineers working at Gwadar Port in May of the same year and, more recently, the abduction of the head of the U.N. refugee agency (an American citizen) in February 2009 from Quetta. Although the Baloch insurgency has been relatively calm over the past year, unrest reignited in the province in early April after the bodies of three top Baloch rebel leaders were discovered in the Turbat area near the Iranian border. The Baloch separatist groups claim that the rebel leaders died at the hands of Pakistani security forces.

The Baloch rebels have no direct quarrel with the United States or NATO member states and are far more interested in attacking Pakistani targets. But they have struck foreign interests before in Balochistan to pressure Islamabad in negotiations. Baloch rebels also demonstrated the ability to strike Western targets in Karachi when they bombed a KFC fast-food restaurant in November 2005. Although the separatists have yet to show any interest in attacking U.S./NATO convoys running through the region, future attacks cannot be ruled out.

The main threat along this route comes from Islamist militants who are active in the final 150-kilometer stretch of the road between the Quetta region and the Chaman border crossing. This section of highway N-25 runs through what is known as the Pashtun corridor in northwest Balochistan, bordering South Waziristan agency on the southern tip of the FATA.

Although the supply route traversing this region has seen very few attacks, the situation could easily change. A number of jihadists who have sought sanctuary from the firefights farther north as well as Afghan Taliban chief Mullah Mohammed Omar and his Quetta Shura (or leadership council) are believed to be hiding in the Quetta area. The Pashtun corridor also is the stronghold of Pakistan's largest Islamist party, the pro-Taliban Jamiat Ulema-i-Islam. In addition, the al Qaeda-linked anti-Shiite group LeJ has been engaged in sectarian and other attacks in the region. Northwestern Balochistan also is a key launch pad for Taliban operations in southern Afghanistan and is the natural extension of Pakistani Taliban activity in the tribal belt. Although the Baloch separatists are firmly secular in their views, they have been energized by the rise of Islamist groups fighting the same enemy: the Pakistani state.

A Worrisome Outlook

The developing U.S. military strategy for Afghanistan suffers from a number of strategic flaws. Chief among them is the fact — and there is no getting around it — that Pakistan serves as the primary supply line for both the Western forces and the jihadist forces fighting each other in Afghanistan.

Pakistan's balancing act between the United States and its former Islamist militant proxies is becoming untenable as many of those proxies turn against the Pakistani state. And as stability deteriorates in Pakistan, the less reliable the landscape is for facilitating the overland shipment of military supplies into Afghanistan. The Russians, meanwhile, are not exactly eager to make life easier for the United States in Afghanistan by cooperating in any meaningful way on alternate supply routes through Central Asia.

Jihadist forces in Pakistan's northwest have already picked up on the idea that the long U.S./NATO supply route through northern Pakistan makes a strategic and vulnerable target in their campaign against the West. Attacks on supply convoys have thus far been concentrated in the volatile tribal badlands along the northwest frontier with Afghanistan. But the Pakistani Taliban are growing bolder by the day and are publicly announcing their intent to spread beyond the Pashtun areas and into the Pakistani core of Punjab. The Pakistani government and military, meanwhile, are strategically stymied. They cannot follow U.S. orders and turn every Pashtun into an enemy, and they cannot afford to see their country crushed under the weight of the jihadists. As a result, the jihadists gain strength while the writ of the Pakistani state erodes.

But the jihadists are not the only ones that CENTCOM should be worrying about as it analyzes its logistical challenges in Pakistan. Islamist sympathizers in Pakistan's security apparatus and organized crime elements can take — and have taken — advantage of the shoddy security infrastructure in place to transport U.S./NATO supplies through the country. In addition, there are secular political forces in play — from the MQM in Karachi to the Baloch rebels in Quetta — that could tip the balance in areas now considered relatively safe for transporting supplies to Afghanistan.

The United States is becoming increasing reliant on Pakistan, just as Pakistan is becoming increasingly unreliable. There are no quick fixes to the problem, but the first step in addressing it is to understand the wide array of threats currently engulfing the Pakistan.

The Implications of Mehsud's Death
Aug. 7, 2009

Unofficial reports released Aug. 7 claimed that an unmanned aerial vehicle (UAV) strike Aug. 5 killed Tehrik-i-Taliban Pakistan (TTP) leader Baitullah Mehsud and his second wife in Laddah, in the Federally Administered Tribal Areas (FATA). The funeral for Mehsud and his wife reportedly has been held in nearby Norgosa. The strike may indicate increasing cooperation between the United

States and Pakistan to address the Islamist militant threat in the Afghanistan-Pakistan region.

Assistance from the United States to eliminate a thorn in Pakistan's side may help efforts to address the Taliban in Afghanistan.

The Aug. 5 UAV strike that allegedly killed Mehsud likely was not carried out by the Pakistanis but by the Americans. Pakistani military forces had been softening up central South Waziristan — from which Mehsud was operating — with fixed-wing, conventional airstrikes, using F-16s and AH-1 Cobra attack helicopters. But U.S. aircraft and UAVs have more advanced weaponry and targeting capabilities and were likely in a better position to respond to such a time-sensitive task. However, such a strike could not occur without quick and accurate intelligence, and Pakistan possesses superior intelligence on Mehsud's whereabouts and movements through human assets on the ground and in the region.

While Mehsud has been a top priority for Pakistan for some time due to his consistent attacks on Pakistani police and military targets, he has only recently become a top priority for the United States. Mehsud's forces have not posed a direct threat to U.S. interests in the region (though he did issue statements that his group would launch attacks against the United States on April 4). But his forces have done a great deal to undermine Pakistani security forces, detracting from their ability to assist the U.S. position in Afghanistan. UAV strikes in the FATA region of Pakistan have only in the past year started targeting Mehsud in earnest, but without much success. Many Pakistani decision makers questioned the motive of U.S. UAV strikes on Pakistani soil in the FATA that killed some midlevel al Qaeda commanders but failed to have a greater impact on Pakistan's burdensome militant problem. Furthermore, these strikes inevitably killed civilians, which hurt Islamabad's ability to support and extend the government's campaign against militants.

However, if Mehsud was indeed targeted and killed by an American UAV, it may help prove to the Pakistanis that the United States can offer concrete help to counter Pakistan's militant threat. It would also be further evidence that U.S. strikes on Pakistani soil have been carried out with the permission of and in coordination with Islamabad.

If the Pakistanis do feel that U.S. assistance played a decisive role in furthering their own ends, it may engender further coordination and cooperation between Washington and Islamabad, including Pakistani support for more U.S. operations against al Qaeda prime and Taliban assets in not only Pakistan but also Afghanistan — to a limited degree. The Taliban movement in Afghanistan is a very poorly understood phenomenon, but if any country understands the dynamics of the movement, it is Pakistan, which was largely responsible for backing the Afghan Taliban. This puts Pakistan in the unique position of being able to provide key intelligence to the United States on Taliban structure, movements and locations. Much of this information is held by Pakistan's Inter-Services Intelligence (ISI) directorate, but if the intelligence that led to the Aug. 5 strike on Mehsud originated in the ISI, it may be a sign that the agency is more willing to share intelligence — and that could have broader implications for the intelligence Pakistan is able to provide to the United States. Such a turn of events could have its origins in the May 27 targeting of ISI offices in Lahore, carried out by Mehsud's forces, an action that certainly would have put pressure on any Taliban sympathizers in the ISI to give up their assets.

This raises the question of how much help this attack will provide to U.S. interests in Afghanistan. Certainly, it disrupts a major threat to Pakistan's internal stability, allowing the Pakistani military to focus on pursuing militants offensively rather than staying on the defensive. But cooperation from the Pakistanis in Afghanistan has been limited so far; the Pakistanis view the Afghan Taliban as an asset they can use to regain influence and are loath to weaken that asset by providing intelligence for U.S. actions. However, many factions of the Afghan Taliban have little or no connection to Pakistan and are also in al Qaeda's camp. The United States will want Pakistan to help with al Qaeda and Afghanistan. Pakistan will help provide information on al Qaeda and Taliban forces linked to them, but the Afghan Taliban with ties to Pakistan will remain an interest that Islamabad will not want to jeopardize.

Therefore, Pakistan will strike a balance between its imperatives and provide intelligence on Afghan Taliban elements linked to al Qaeda, which are not under Pakistan's influence and can help Islamabad better manage the Afghan Taliban landscape and Pakistan's domestic security. The assistance that Islamabad may give could also help the United States in its efforts to level the battlefield and its attempts to distinguish between reconcilable Taliban (those who do not harm Pakistani interests) and irreconcilable Taliban (those who do). Islamabad and Washington will likely share intelligence on Taliban factions that are a problem for both Pakistan and the United States and have ties to al Qaeda. Conversely, Pakistan is unlikely to be willing to give up intelligence on the groups upon which it has influence (that is, good intelligence) because it considers them an important operational asset.

The killing of Mehsud may actually embolden the Pakistanis, since it would mark a weakening of those Taliban factions that oppose Pakistan. With more confidence in its influence over the remaining Taliban elements, Pakistan could be even less willing to sell out its Taliban assets in Afghanistan. Commanders such as Maulvi Nazir (in South Waziristan) and Hafiz Gul Bahadir (in North Waziristan) have tended to align themselves with Taliban forces in eastern Afghanistan and have largely avoided attacking Pakistani assets (unlike Mehsud), and so have not been under as much scrutiny from Pakistani security forces. Mehsud's death could tilt the control of Taliban activity to commanders such as these. As long as they continue to avoid attacks in Pakistan and focus on Afghanistan, Pakistan would have little interest in confronting them. But the complex mix of loyalties on both sides of the border remains a fact of life for the United States, NATO and Pakistan.

A New Approach to Afghanistan
Feb. 2, 2010

Pakistani army chief Gen. Ashfaq Kayani said Feb. 2 that when Pakistan wants Afghanistan to be in its strategic depth, this does not imply controlling Afghanistan. He added that "if Afghanistan is peaceful, stable and friendly, we have our strategic depth because our western border is secure." Kayani went on to point out that Pakistan does not want a Talibanized Afghanistan, saying "we can't wish for anything for Afghanistan that we don't wish for ourselves."

The statements — a first for a Pakistani leader — reveal an emerging shift in Islamabad's thinking about Afghanistan and the Taliban.

Pakistan has long been interested in Afghan politics, since a key Pakistani strategic imperative is being the most influential player in Afghanistan. This is to help ensure that Pakistan is not surrounded by India on one side and a pro-New Delhi Afghan state on the other. After decades of trying to achieve this imperative, Pakistan finally succeeded when the Taliban came to power in the 1990s. This proved short-lived; after 9/11, Pakistan lost its influence — something Islamabad has sought to regain ever since. To do so, Islamabad had to balance maintaining influence over the Taliban against the need to ally with Washington in the jihadist war. But in the end, this proved to be an untenable tightrope walk as the process led to the emergence of a Pakistani Taliban phenomenon.

STRATFOR has pointed for some time to Pakistan's growing post-Sept. 11 strategic dilemma — namely, how can Islamabad balance a domestic policy of fighting its own Pakistani Taliban rebels against a foreign policy of maintaining influence in Afghanistan by supporting the Afghan Taliban? While the Pakistani and Afghan Taliban may divide into two neat categories on paper, ground realities are much messier. Having al Qaeda in the mix further muddies these waters. Ultimately, Pakistan failed at its balancing act. It lost control over the jihadist landscape within its own borders, which in turn undermined its ability to project power into Afghanistan.

Kayani's statements highlight the manner in which Pakistan is trying to deal with this problem. The Pakistani army chief has hinted that Islamabad does not want to see Afghanistan be dominated by the Afghan Taliban. He did not, however, comment on the possibility that Pakistan could use its links with the Afghan Taliban to push it toward peace talks, which is a function of Islamabad not wanting to show its cards just yet and/or the dearth of such cards.

Pakistan's shift away from wanting to see the Afghan Taliban dominate Afghanistan to supporting a more broad-based Afghan government in which the Taliban constitute a key component is significant. It stems from Pakistani fears that Taliban control of Afghanistan (which Pakistan saw as a good thing from the 1990s until only recently) could prove deadly to Pakistani security. Pakistan now has decided that the best way to check Indian influence in Afghanistan — which has grown considerably over the past eight years — is to forge ties beyond the Taliban, and even beyond the Pashtun community.

This shift is still very much in the making, and it will certainly face resistance in Pakistan. While the leadership of the army-intelligence establishment has come to terms with the need for the shift, it will be a while before the establishment as a whole embraces the new approach. If successful, the shift could bring the U.S. and Pakistani regional calculus closer.

The discrepancy between Islamabad's good-versus-bad Taliban and Washington's reconcilable-versus-irreconcilable Taliban has long been obvious to STRATFOR. Islamabad's incipient embrace of the idea that a Talibanized Afghanistan is not in Pakistani interests indicates that the U.S.-Pakistani divide on the Taliban could be lessened. Kayani alluded to as much when he said that the world could help the process by having "a proper understanding" of Pakistan's concerns and issues, adding that the United States and other nations have only a short-term interest in Afghanistan, while for Pakistan, the war in Afghanistan "is our war and not the U.S. war." In other words, geography will allow the United States to forget about Afghanistan in a few years — an option Pakistan lacks.

169

Pakistan now appears ready to settle for less than it originally sought in Afghanistan. Rather than seeking to be the lead player in Afghanistan, Islamabad will settle for an Afghan regime that does not threaten its security and other interests, similar to how the Iranians ultimately settled for less in Iraq once they accepted that Iraq was not about to fall in their lap after the U.S. invasion.

Beyond Negotiations With the Afghan Taliban
Feb. 4, 2010

Wednesday marked a significant milestone in U.S. efforts to bring closure to Afghanistan's jihadist war. For the first time, a top American general issued two key statements that herald a major shift in the way the United States will be dealing with the Taliban insurgency in Afghanistan. One pertained to Pakistan's role in combating the regional jihadist war while another focused on negotiations with the Afghan Taliban.

In an interview with Reuters, U.S. Central Command head Gen. David Petraeus said that the Pakistani military, at the present time, has reached a limit regarding the scope of the counterinsurgency campaign on its side of the border. This is a major shift from the eight-year stance that Pakistan needed to "do more" in terms of aggressive action against Islamist militants. More important, Gen. Petraeus spoke of the need for Islamabad to play a key role in bringing the Afghan Taliban to the negotiating table, given the historic links between Pakistan's army-intelligence establishment and the jihadist movement. This also signals that the gulf between the American and Pakistani view of the Afghan Taliban is on its way to being bridged.

The most noteworthy comment from the top U.S. commander, however, was his remark that it was too soon to hope for reconciliation with the likes of Afghan Taliban leader Mullah Omar, though negotiations with senior Taliban leaders could not be ruled out. This statement represents a major course correction. Until these remarks were published by Reuters on Wednesday, the American position on negotiations was that they would take place only with pragmatic Afghan Taliban elements who could be separated from the core of the movement. Talking to the senior leadership of the Afghan Taliban and Pakistani involvement in the process go hand in hand given that Islamabad is the one player that can facilitate such an engagement.

These shifts seem to confirm what STRATFOR said last week in this same forum: When all is said and done, the Afghan jihadist movement — in one form or another — will be part of the government in Kabul. Given the trend line, it is no longer premature to begin thinking about what such a government would look like. To a great degree, the answer to this question lies in understanding the true power of the Taliban and their strategic calculus moving forward.

Publicly, Taliban leaders will continue to reiterate their hard-line position that they will not negotiate until Western forces have exited their country. But they know the reach of their upper hand on the battlefield; they are not without limits of their own. The Taliban are well aware that the anarchic conditions that allowed them to steam-roll into Kabul in the 1990s no longer exist.

In the past eight years, enough arresters have emerged for the price of regaining what the Taliban lost (control over roughly 90 percent of the country) in the wake of the 9/11 attacks to be a major civil war that could not result in the jihadists crushing their opponents. The Afghan jihadists also remember how they unsuccessfully sought international recognition for their regime between 1996 and 2001, and they realize that now more than ever they will need to be recognized as a legitimate entity. This is why we see them telegraphing to the international community that they have no transnational ambitions beyond Afghanistan's borders.

We have talked about how the Taliban have an eventual major interest in engaging in negotiations, which was confirmed a few days ago when one of their spokesmen did not categorically reject the notion of talks (saying the leadership would soon decide upon it). What this means is that while they would prefer to be able to re-establish single-party rule in the country, they are likely to settle for a coalition government in which they have the dominant position because they happen to be the most powerful political force in the country's largest ethnic group. It should be noted that a few days ago, Pakistan — which wields the most influence over the Afghan Taliban — also openly opposed the idea of a Talibanized Afghanistan.

While there are tremendous differences in the ground realities between Iraq and Afghanistan, it appears that the Taliban could end up in a position similar to that of the Iraqi Shia; they may not enjoy a monopoly on power but they would hold most of the cards. Of course, there is always the possibility that any such arrangement will not hold in the long run, as is the risk in Iraq, which has a far more evolved political system than Afghanistan. As a result, the Taliban and their opponents may return to the old-fashioned way of settling power struggles and engage in a prolonged civil war. But if there is to be a settlement prior to the departure of Western forces, it will not be one that would allow the Taliban to single-handedly impose a writ on the country.

A Shift in Dealing With the Afghan Taliban?
Feb. 19, 2010

Pakistani security officials announced Feb. 18 that Mohammed Haqqani, son of Jalaluddin and brother of Sirajuddin Haqqani (who leads the Taliban in eastern Afghanistan), was killed in an unmanned aerial vehicle (UAV) missile strike the same day. Mohammed Haqqani's role within the Haqqani network is unclear, and even his death is being contradicted by some STRATFOR sources (confirming the death is all but impossible, given the difficulty of obtaining forensic evidence from the scene), but his presumed demise is not likely to seriously affect the group's operations.

However, the strike targeting Mohammed Haqqani could be linked to the nascent shift in U.S.-Pakistani dealings on Afghanistan. The United States has long pursued Haqqani family members and associates in North Waziristan, part of Pakistan's tribal belt, using UAV missile strikes. Washington considers the Haqqani network as irreconcilable Taliban, due to the network's close ties to al Qaeda. The success of the Feb. 18 strike has prompted speculation that the intelligence preceding the attack came from Pakistan.

Pakistan has worked with the United States for some time in targeting al Qaeda and the Tehrik-i-Taliban Pakistan in the tribal areas, but it has avoided acting against the Haqqanis and other Pakistani Taliban elements that fight in Afghanistan. Pakistani leaders believe they need the Haqqanis, and the wider Afghan Taliban movement, to exert influence in Afghanistan — a strategic geopolitical imperative for Pakistan.

However, Mohammed Haqqani's presumed death comes in the context of a major, unprecedented move by the Pakistanis to crack down on the Afghan Taliban. Earlier in February, Pakistan arrested the Afghan Taliban's second-in-command, Mullah Baradar, in a raid on a house in Karachi. While few details are known about this arrest (it is not even clear whether it was an arrest or a ruse; he appears to be in custody but the exact circumstances are unclear), it appears to be an example of Pakistan's increasing aggressiveness toward the Afghan Taliban.

The alleged killing of Mohammad Haqqani and arrest of Baradar appear to be much more in line with the United States' interests than in Pakistan's interests in Afghanistan. Right now, Washington and Islamabad are relying on each other heavily: The United States needs Pakistani assistance to wrap up the military mission in Afghanistan, while Pakistan is interested in working with the United States to eliminate Afghan Taliban elements that are not in line with Pakistani strategy. In fact, if Pakistan is indeed involved in the move against the Haqqani network, this interest in eliminating some Afghan Taliban could be the reason for it.

Pakistan is interested in hiving off al Qaeda from the Haqqani network in order to convince the United States that the Haqqani network is in fact a reconcilable faction of the Taliban. By surgically removing certain elements of the Haqqani-al Qaeda relationship, Pakistan could achieve this. Pakistan has already arrested one of the Haqqani brothers in order to contain the family and keep the Haqqanis' al Qaeda connections from undermining Pakistan's interests. This strategy would be in keeping with Pakistan's need to align its distinction of good and bad Taliban with the U.S. dichotomy of reconcilable and irreconcilable Taliban.

Since few details are available and confirmations are pending, it is not certain that the alleged killing of Mohammed Haqqani and the alleged arrest of a top Afghan Taliban leader are indeed part of this strategy. But these two developments certainly signal that relations between the United States and Pakistan bear watching as the countries attempt to come to terms on how to address Afghanistan and reach a consensus on which factions of the Taliban can stay and which should be removed.

A Reality Check on the Quetta Shura Arrests
Feb. 25, 2010

Seven of the 15 members of the so-called Quetta Shura, the Afghan Taliban's shadowy apex leadership council based in the Pashtun corridor of Pakistan's Balochistan province, have been arrested, according to a Feb. 24 report in The Christian Science Monitor, a U.S. newspaper, citing unnamed Pakistani intelligence officials. In addition to the previously reported arrests of Mullah Abdul Ghani Baradar, Maulavi Abdul Kabir and Mullah Muhammad Younis, the article said Mullah Abdul Qayoum Zakir, who oversees the movement's military affairs, Mullah Muhammad Hassan, Mullah Ahmed Jan Akhunzada and Mullah Abdul Raouf also have been detained.

Only about half of these arrests have been confirmed so far. But more important, the composition of the Quetta Shura is itself a closely guarded secret. Only Pakistan's Directorate of Inter-Services Intelligence (ISI) has the sophisticated and nuanced understanding of the Afghan Taliban to even have a good grasp of the council's membership, so reports from unnamed officials are extremely difficult to verify. No one has a master list of the Afghan Taliban leadership with which to check off individuals.

Even if all these men have indeed been arrested, it is difficult to say whether the Quetta Shura has really been reduced significantly, or if the individuals arrested are actually those they are thought to be. Almost all reports on the details of the arrests cite Pakistani security officials, and there is no way to independently verify them. Islamabad has incentive to show that it is cooperating with the United States while it reshapes the Afghan Taliban leadership landscape to suit its own long-term purposes.

This most recent leak comes as Pakistan publicizes a string of Pakistani intelligence coups ranging from the arrest of shadow Taliban governors from northern Afghanistan to the death of the leader of Lashkar e Jhangvi (LeJ), Qari Zafar, to Pakistan's supporting role in the Iranian arrest of Abdolmalek Rigi, the leader of Jundallah. Many aspects of these reports cannot be verified at this time, and given the lack of corroboration and Pakistan's interests in manipulating perceptions, there is much to suggest that at least some elements in Islamabad are feeding the media for their own purposes.

There are at least partial truths in this series of reports, and there is no doubt that some significant achievements have been made. Baradar, for example, appears to be in Pakistani custody and may soon be transferred to a detention facility at Bagram Air Base north of Kabul.

But there are a number of moving parts in the attempts to negotiate with the Taliban — or degrade their capabilities. Pakistan is playing a complex game, and one important question is the extent to which Pakistan is indeed cooperating and coordinating with the United States in a meaningful way, rather than simply making temporary or symbolic gestures. The Pakistanis are deeply skeptical of U.S. support in the long run, and they already are thinking about managing Afghanistan when the United States begins to draw down there in coming years.

However, there is a chapter of history to be written before that happens, and Pakistan has every intention of being at the center of any negotiations with the Afghan Taliban, including the talks, the reconciliation process and the implementation of a settlement. A spate of arrests like those of the Quetta Shura members — regardless of whether they actually have been taken out of commission — may indicate that some sort of power play is taking place. But such a development cannot be presently confirmed, and Islamabad has no shortage of reasons to manipulate perceptions.

The Pakistani Strategy in Afghanistan
March 17, 2010

The Pakistani strategy of securing influence in Afghanistan is dictated by the unalterable reality of geography. With a long common border, a strong Pashtun population on both sides and active militant groups interconnected with each other across the border, Pakistan is forced to take an active role in Afghanistan. It's the same sort of geopolitical imperative that bound the colonial British to the region, and before them the Muslim emperors, and before the Muslim emperors the Hindu rulers.

Pakistan's core is comprised of the provinces of Punjab and Sindh, which encompass the country's demographic, industrial, commercial and agricultural base. From Punjab in the north, this heartland extends southward through Sindh province, flowing seamlessly along the Indus River valley into the Thar Desert. This means Pakistan's core is hard by the Indian border, leaving no meaningful terrain barriers to invasion. (Indeed, the Punjabi population straddles the

Indian-Pakistani border much as the Pashtun population straddles the Pakistani-Afghan border.) This narrow strip of flat land is inherently vulnerable to India, Pakistan's arch-rival to the east, a geographic arrangement that was no accident of the British partition.

Suffering from both geographic and demographic disadvantages vis-à-vis India — and with no strategic depth to speak of — Pakistan is extremely anxious about its security in the east and is forced to look in the opposite direction both out of concern for its depth and in search of opportunity.

West of the Punjabi-Sindhi core lay the peripheral territories of the North-West Frontier Province (NWFP), Federally Administered Tribal Areas (FATA) and Balochistan province. Though the Pakistani buffer territories of the NWFP and FATA are far more interlinked with Afghanistan than with Pakistan by virtue of the common Pashtun populations, they do provide Pakistan with some of the depth it lacks to the east and also protect against encroachment from the northwest. Having firm control of its own heartland and secure access to the sea through the port of Karachi, Islamabad must also control these buffer territories as a means of further consolidating security in the Punjabi-Sindhi core.

In this effort, Afghanistan is both part of the problem and part of the solution. It is part of the problem because the Islamist insurgency that Islamabad once supported in Afghanistan has now spilled backwards onto Pakistani soil; it is part of the solution because Afghanistan remains a critical geopolitical arena for Islamabad. By securing itself as the single most dominant player in Afghanistan, Pakistan strengthens its hand in its own peripheral territories and ensures that no other foreign power — India is the immediate concern here — ever gains a foothold in Kabul. If India did, it would have Pakistan more or less surrounded. Indeed, the need to assert influence in Afghanistan is hardwired into Pakistan's geopolitical makeup.

History

Afghanistan already was an issue for Pakistan when the Soviets invaded Afghanistan in the final days of 1979. A secular Marxist government was in Kabul supported by arch-rival India and bent on eradicating the influence of religion (a powerful and important aspect of Pakistani influence in Afghanistan). When the Soviets invaded, Pakistan used Saudi money and U.S. arms to back a seven-party Islamist alliance. In the civil war that followed the Soviet withdrawal, Pakistan threw its support behind the much more hard-line Islamist Taliban and gave it the training and tools it needed to rise up and eventually take control of most of the country. Though Afghanistan was still chaotic, it was the kind of Islamist chaos that the Pakistanis could manage — that is, until Sept. 11, 2001, and the American invasion to topple the Taliban regime for providing sanctuary to al Qaeda.

Thus ensued an almost impossible tightrope walk by the government of then-President Gen. Pervez Musharraf. Pakistan was forced to abruptly end support for the Taliban regime it had helped put into power and around which its strategy for retaining influence in Afghanistan revolved. Islamabad tried to play both sides, retaining contact with the Taliban but also providing the United States with intelligence that helped U.S. forces hunt the Taliban. This engendered distrust on both sides in the process. The Taliban realized that they could not depend on or trust Pakistan as they once did, and from 2003 to 2006, American pressure on Islamabad to crack down on al Qaeda in Pakistan's tribal areas directly contributed to the rise of the Pakistani Taliban.

So as the Islamist insurgency in Afghanistan spilled backwards into Pakistan, the cross-border Taliban phenomenon began to include groups focused on the destruction of the Pakistani state. To this day, however, despite the inextricably linked nature of these Pashtun Islamists, there is still an inclination within many quarters in Islamabad to distinguish between the "good" Taliban, who have their sights set on Afghanistan and ultimately Kabul (and with whom Pakistan retains significant, if reduced, influence), and the

178

"bad" Taliban, who have become fixated on the regime in Islamabad and have perpetrated attacks against Pakistani targets. There also are other, non-Pashtun renegade Islamist elements that have carried out major attacks beyond Pakistani borders that have risked provoking Indian aggression, such as the militant attack in Mumbai in 2008.

Nevertheless, Pakistan has realized that the militant problem in Afghanistan has endangered the weak control it does have over the buffer territories of the FATA and NWFP and is applying military force to the problem on its side of the border. It also appears to be working closer with the United States in terms of sharing intelligence. Across the border in Afghanistan, Pakistan does not want to see the Taliban stage too strong a comeback because of the offshoots of the movement that are becoming problematic on Pakistan's own turf.

Strategy

But the Afghan Taliban can neither be ignored nor destroyed. They still have utility for Islamabad and must be dealt with. This will require skillful handling on the part of the Pakistanis, who have lost a lot of leverage over the group. Islamabad's strategy is to try and balance a domestic policy that seeks to militarily neutralize Taliban rebels on the Pakistani side of the border while working with the Taliban on the Afghan side to achieve its foreign policy aims. Pakistan's intelligence service, the Inter-Services Intelligence directorate, can provide devastating intelligence on the Taliban movement to the Americans, giving Islamabad leverage over Washington. And its long-standing connections to the group put Islamabad in a unique position to facilitate and oversee any negotiated settlement.

So Pakistan is seeking to maximize its influence within the Afghan Taliban movement, gain ownership of any negotiation efforts and be recognized internationally as the single most important player in Afghanistan. The West's interest in withdrawing from Afghanistan puts Pakistan in a good position to succeed here. The Americans know

Pakistan must be part of the solution and are anxious for Islamabad to provide that solution.

But to succeed, Pakistan must again walk the middle ground between the United States and the Taliban. And once it is at the center of the negotiations, it must not only push both parties toward each other, it must also pull them in a third direction in order to satisfy its own aims — namely, to establish long-term conditions for Pakistani domination over Afghanistan.

And to succeed in this effort, Pakistan will need more than just the Taliban. It must establish influence with the other key players in Afghanistan — particularly the government of President Hamid Karzai, who recently acknowledged that Islamabad will have a great deal of influence in the country but that he wishes to place limits on it as much as possible. And this is where things get tricky. The United States may ultimately have no choice but to work with Pakistan in attempting to secure a negotiated settlement with reconcilable elements of the Taliban. But Karzai is also seeking a deal with the Taliban, and if he can achieve one outside of Pakistan's influence, he can try and minimize Pakistani influence in the negotiations (though Pakistan can no more be cut out of the negotiations than could the Taliban).

At the same time, Islamabad must find common ground with other regional players — Iran, Saudi Arabia and Turkey — in order to roll back Indian influence in Afghanistan (there even appears to be an emerging axis of sorts consisting of the Americans, the Saudis and the Turks). But Russian Prime Minister Vladimir Putin visited New Delhi March 11 in order to coordinate and craft a common strategy for Afghanistan — a strategy being formulated between two countries that share a common interest in Afghanistan that runs counter to Pakistan's and is coming closer to aligning with Iran's.

In sum, Pakistan retains more levers in Afghanistan than any other single country, and with Saudi money and American might it is maneuvering to be the pivotal player in a powerful coalition with abundant resources. But Pakistan will continue to face challenges as it tries to distinguish between and divide the Taliban phenomenon in Afghanistan and within its own borders.

CHAPTER 5: OTHER PLAYERS

Why Indian-Afghan Cooperation is a Problem for Pakistan
April 11, 2008

The Indian army will train Afghanistan's army in counterinsurgency operations — the latest development in a growing alliance between India and Afghanistan that threatens the country sandwiched in-between: Pakistan. For Pakistan, it would appear that this triangular relationship is coming full circle.

Afghanistan's Defense Minister Abdul Rahim Wardak met with his Indian counterpart A. K. Antony in the Indian capital April 10 to discuss bilateral military cooperation, the Associated Press of Pakistan reported April 11. While the Indian defense minister ruled out any military involvement in Afghanistan, the increased cooperation between New Delhi and Kabul puts Pakistan in a weakened position with its neighbors.

Wardak also visited the 15th Corps of the Indian army, headquartered in Srinagar, the capital of Indian-administered Kashmir, and will visit the Indian air force's training command and Hindustan Aeronautics Limited in Bangalore in southern India. These visits are coming amid reports that Afghanistan might be considering sending its air force pilots to India for training. Wardak said his country would seek New Delhi's help in maintaining Soviet-era helicopter

181

gunships and medium helicopters to provide logistical support to its armed forces. NATO can also use the increased interest in Indian involvement in counterterrorism efforts as leverage against Pakistan to rein in militants on its soil.

India and Afghanistan are pushing the idea that the faster India trains the Afghan army, the quicker NATO can withdraw troops from Afghanistan. India's goal is to gain a toehold in the Afghan military establishment, creating goodwill that it can cash in when the time comes. This prospect worries Pakistan, which sees India as its biggest rival. Antony assured Wardak that India would remain "actively engaged" in the reconstruction and rehabilitation of war-wrecked Afghanistan.

While it will be some time before the relationship between the Indian and Afghan militaries is solidified in any meaningful way, even the meager assistance India provides Afghanistan is a significant enhancement of its military involvement, which until now has been mostly related to reconstruction and development work in Afghanistan. New Delhi's key interest in Afghanistan has to do with its security vis-à-vis its neighboring rival, Pakistan, and the transnational Islamist militant groups headquartered in Pakistan.

To best understand the impact of India's growing support in Afghanistan, one must understand Pakistan's recent history of backing Islamist militant groups and how Pakistan has tried to use Afghanistan to gain strategic advantage against India. Long before the Soviet intervention in Afghanistan during the 1980s, Islamabad viewed Kabul as being aligned with New Delhi. Pakistan felt sandwiched between its archrival to the east and a hostile regime to the west. Another issue was that secular left-leaning Pakistani Pashtun forces were pushing for a separate homeland for their ethnic group — a demand backed by Afghanistan in those days.

To deal with these threats, the Pakistanis decided to employ the Islamist card to counter Pashtun nationalism on both sides of the Durand Line — the boundary drawn in 1893 that divides the Pashtun people and remains a source of tension between the governments of Afghanistan and Pakistan. Even before 1977, when the

Islamist-leaning regime of Gen. Muhammad Zia-ul-Haq came to power, the Pakistanis had aligned themselves with Afghan Islamist dissidents such as Gulbuddin Hekmatyar. Then came the Soviet intervention in Afghanistan in 1979, when Islamabad's backing of Afghan Islamists increased, with the support of the United States and Saudi Arabia. By the time the Soviets withdrew in defeat from Afghanistan a decade later, the Pakistanis had successfully contained ethnic Pashtun nationalism. They had also unwittingly sown the seeds of jihadism, which would bite the hand of its creator years later.

The Soviet withdrawal from Afghanistan provided the Pakistanis the opportunity to direct their attention to Indian-administered Kashmir, the disputed region on the border that Pakistan has long sought to control. A separatist rising in Kashmir gave Pakistan a chance to play a new hand in its same Islamist militant strategy. As early as the 1947-1948 India-Pakistan War, the Pakistanis employed Pashtun tribesmen in its bid to seize control of the parts of Kashmir that are now under Pakistani administration.

In 1996, the Pakistani military realized its objective of installing a pro-Islamabad regime in Kabul when it supported the Taliban, the extremist Islamist movement that controlled Afghanistan until the U.S.-backed coalition drove them from power after Sept. 11, 2001. Pakistan had hoped that with its rear flank secure it could then deal with India, especially in the context of Kashmir, which it unsuccessfully tried to do in the Kargil mini-war in 1999. Between the failure of the Kargil operation and the events of 9/11, Pakistan lost its ability to project power into Kashmir and Afghanistan. The Pakistanis also began to lose control over the Islamist militant landscape with the rise of al Qaeda, which brought together the various strands of militant forces that threatened both Kabul and New Delhi.

Thus, Pakistan opened a process of normalization with India and began cooperating to some extent with Washington against al Qaeda while continuing to maintain an ambiguous stance toward the Taliban. That was because the Pashtun jihadist movement was the only available card Islamabad could play as it pursued its interests in Afghanistan and sought to keep India out. By offering economic and developmental assistance to Afghan President Hamid Karzai's government, India was able to establish some influence, which alarmed the Pakistanis. Even so, Islamabad was able to take comfort in knowing that it had an asset in the insurgent Taliban, which it could use to block Indian moves in Afghanistan.

However, things have changed. The relationship between Islamabad and the Afghan Taliban has been complicated by the raise of the Taliban in Pakistan. And with the complex nature of Pakistan's alignment with the United States and the gravitation of jihadist forces toward al Qaeda, Islamabad no longer has an effective response to India's plans for counterinsurgency cooperation with Afghanistan. Pakistan's ability to counter India's moves has been further weakened by a coalition government — formed by foes of President Pervez Musharraf — sweeping parliamentary elections and by the fact that Musharraf no longer heads the military. If, at some point, the Taliban gain a larger share of power in Afghanistan, Pakistani influence would be limited because of the break between the Taliban and Islamabad.

With the Taliban no longer in the Pakistani camp as they once were, Afghanistan could return to being hostile to Pakistan. There is significant anti-Pakistani sentiment in Afghanistan because of the perception of Pakistani interference in the country's business. Indeed, Afghan attitudes in general are far more positive toward India because of the increased assistance India has begun to provide.

The Taliban's Break With Al Qaeda
Oct. 7, 2008

More details emerged Oct. 6 about British-backed talks that Afghanistan and its Western allies held recently with representatives of the Taliban in Saudi Arabia. The talks, hosted by Saudi King Abdullah himself, were held Sept. 24-27 in Mecca and involved 11 Taliban delegates, two Afghan government officials, a representative of Islamist rebel leader Gulbuddin Hekmatyar and three others. The report also quoted an unnamed source as saying that Taliban leader Mullah Mohammad Omar has made it clear he is no longer allied with al Qaeda.

The recent surge in backchannel activity as well as increasing international interest in talks with the Taliban would not have been possible without Afghan President Hamid Karzai's government — and, more important, its Western backers — having some degree of confidence that Omar and his associates in the Taliban hierarchy were prepared to part ways with al Qaeda. In fact, many factors — including geography and diverging interests — might have already put significant distance between the leaderships of the Taliban and al Qaeda prime.

From an operational security perspective, it would have been very difficult for the two leaderships to have maintained close contact since the fall of the Taliban regime in late 2001, particularly since they are in two different parts of Pakistan. Omar likely is in the Pashtun corridor of Balochistan province and al Qaeda leaders Osama bin Laden and Ayman al-Zawahiri likely are in the Dir/Malakand region. Moreover, as STRATFOR discussed two years ago, the Afghan Taliban movement has splintered into three broad categories. There are Taliban forces linked to Omar but based in Afghanistan engaged in the fighting, Taliban elements allied with Pakistan, and Taliban fighters connected to al Qaeda (some might have ties to all three).

Then there are the issues of power and ideology. Though Western officials are just now coming out publicly and acknowledging that a military solution cannot be imposed on Afghanistan, STRATFOR — in keeping with its geopolitical paradigm — has stated that neither a robust central state in Kabul nor a great foreign power militarily controlling the country is possible. STRATFOR has also long believed that ultimately there will be a negotiated settlement with a new leadership that will retain its ideology but within the confines of the Afghan nation-state and will abandon not just al Qaeda but also its transnational objectives of a supranational caliphate.

Omar and his allies have realized this and likely have started gradually repositioning themselves to enhance their chances of a return to power. The Taliban leadership knows it paid a heavy price — its regime — for its unwillingness to part ways with al Qaeda. The Taliban leaders have also noted that al Qaeda has lost appeal among the locals and they realize that if they do not change, they could be sidelined by more pragmatic elements.

In many ways, al Qaeda's jihadist vision never really took root in Afghanistan, given the theological and cultural differences between the jihadists and the Afghans (al Qaeda had the same difficulties in Iraq). In fact, it never really went too far in Saudi Arabia (the birth-place of bin Laden and of jihadism's precursor, Salafism). Riyadh's ability to significantly neutralize jihadists at home has given the Saudis great influence over the Taliban's thinking.

But there are other reasons behind Saudi Arabia's desire to get so heavily and directly involved in talks with the Taliban. The Saudis have an interest in laying bin Laden and the core al Qaeda group to rest. Furthermore, Pakistan — which used to work in tandem with the Saudis on the Taliban issue — is in disarray. With Islamabad fighting its own Taliban insurgency, the Saudis have taken the lead in Afghanistan. It is also quite likely that the Pakistanis need the Saudis to use not only their financial clout but also their political clout with Washington as relations between Islamabad and Washington deteriorate.

Most important, however, is Saudi Arabia's core foreign policy objective: countering the rise of regional rival Iran. Riyadh has seen how Tehran has gained the upper hand in Iraq and is interested in other ways to contain Iran. Afghanistan, with whom Iran shares an extensive land border, gives the Saudis such an opportunity. The Saudis are also aware of the threats posed by the Iranians' extensive influence on their eastern neighbor and even among elements of the Taliban.

Therefore, facilitating a new power-sharing arrangement in which the Taliban return to power in significant ways could serve as a major check on growing Iranian regional influence. Saudi Arabia already

OTHER PLAYERS

has Pakistan as a regional ally and has used it to block Iran from expanding its influence eastward. With the return of the Taliban to the corridors of power in Kabul, Riyadh hopes to reverse the inroads Tehran has made there during the last seven years. Put differently, Southwest Asia is once again about to become an arena for a Saudi-Iranian proxy struggle.

Iran's Interest in a Revived Northern Alliance
March 21, 2009

Iranian Foreign Minister Manouchehr Mottaki arrived March 20 in the northwestern Afghan city of Mazar-e-Sharif to meet with his Afghan and Tajik counterparts in a ceremony marking Nowruz — the Persian New Year celebrated by Iranians, Tajiks, Kurds and Azeris. On the same day, U.S. President Barack Obama sent a message to Iran on the occasion of Nowruz as part of his administration's efforts to engage Tehran diplomatically.

The Iranians have welcomed the "Happy Nowruz" message from Obama, but have reiterated their demand that the United States move beyond statements and take concrete steps to initiate the process of normalizing relations. Tehran knows that Washington is simultaneously trying to reach out to the clerical regime while pursuing a diplomatic approach toward the Taliban, an enemy of Tehran that the Iranians nearly went to war with in 1998. From the Iranian point of view, this is the perfect time to demonstrate to the Americans that in addition to the Middle East, the Persian Islamist regime has great influence in South and Central Asia as well.

Interestingly, the regional gathering is not being held in the Afghan capital, Kabul, but in Mazar-e-Sharif — a city with a Tajik majority in a predominantly Uzbek region near the borders of the Central Asian states (Turkmenistan, Uzbekistan and Tajikistan). It is also the same city where the Taliban murdered 10 diplomats and an

187

Iranian journalist at the Iranian Consulate in August 1998 as part of a larger massacre of Shiite opponents in and around the town after the Taliban re-captured it from the Northern Alliance. Ethnic Tajiks, Uzbeks, Hazara and Turkmen in Afghanistan, along with their allies in Ashgabat, Tashkent and Dushanbe, all share Iran's deep concern over the Taliban resurgence. These state and non-state actors, along with Russia, Iran and India, cooperated in supporting the Northern Alliance (a coalition of Afghan minorities) to counter the Taliban from 1994 to 2001 and then played an instrumental role in the fall of the Taliban regime in the aftermath of 9/11.

Tehran has strong influence among Afghanistan's largest minority group, the Tajiks, because of ethno-linguistic ties. Similarly, it enjoys close relations with the Hazara, who are — like the Iranians — Shia. Given the way the Taliban routed the Northern Alliance in the 1990s, the Iranians understand that they will need to put together a more robust alliance comprising the Afghan minorities. The Uzbeks, however, are key in this regard because after the Tajiks they are the next-largest ethnic group in the country. Moreover, the Uzbeks under the leadership of former military commander Gen. Abdul Rashid Dostum played a key role in the ouster of the Marxist regime in 1992 after defecting to the Islamist rebel alliance.

Therefore, in addition to showing off their regional influence, the Iranians are likely attempting to revive the Northern Alliance. In April 2007, STRATFOR discussed the likelihood of the re-creation of the north-south divide in Afghanistan, pitting its Pashtun majority against the country's minorities. By countering the rise of the Taliban, the Iranians would be offsetting the moves of their main regional rival, Saudi Arabia. Riyadh is interested in seeing the return of the Taliban as a means of checking Iran, which has created problems for Riyadh in the Arab world. Just as Iran has relied on its Arab Shiite allies and other radical forces in the Middle East to expand its influence, the Iranians have ample tools on their eastern front.

Iran is not the only power that has an interest in bolstering the Northern Alliance. The Russians also want to keep the Taliban contained and would have an interest in undermining U.S. strategy in

Afghanistan by reinforcing the Taliban's biggest rivals. Iran will probably work through Russia to create a regional alliance against the Taliban, though Iran is aware that Moscow does not want Iran to expand its influence in Central Asia because the Russians see that region as their exclusive turf.

Additionally, Iran can rely on India to join this anti-Taliban regional alliance because of New Delhi's interest in countering the Taliban's main state-actor ally, Pakistan, and countering the Islamist militant threat that India faces from its western rival. The Indians have openly criticized U.S. efforts to seek out "moderate" Taliban and are bitter about the Obama administration's soft approach toward Islamabad.

This emerging alignment of forces complicates an already complex and difficult situation that the United States faces in dealing with the Taliban and their al Qaeda allies. Washington is struggling to deal with the spread of the jihadist insurgency from Afghanistan to Pakistan and now will have to balance between Iran and Saudi Arabia as it seeks to deal with the Taliban. A revitalization of an anti-Taliban alliance of state and non-state actors will create problems for the U.S. efforts to negotiate with the Taliban.

Such an anti-Taliban coalition also complicates U.S./NATO efforts to reach out to the Central Asian republics and Russia in its search for alternative supply routes. Moscow and the Central Asian states are in favor, at the right price, of allowing the West to ship supplies through their territories to NATO forces in Afghanistan because they also want the Taliban in check. Washington's moves to talk to the Taliban, however, are a cause of concern for the Kremlin and the countries of Central Asia, which is why they will be asking for a role in the U.S.-Iranian negotiations.

These complex dealings underscore the problems that the United States will be facing as it seeks simultaneously to negotiate with its two principal opponents in the Islamic world — Iran and the jihadists.

Turkey's Strategic Outlook on Afghanistan
Dec. 4, 2009

Late on Dec. 3, Turkey rejected a U.S. request to its NATO allies to send more troops to Afghanistan as part of the new U.S. Afghan strategy unveiled by U.S. President Barack Obama on Dec 1. Noting that Ankara had already increased its contingent by a little under a thousand troops in November, Turkish Defense Minister Vecdi Gonul said Turkey was not going to change its policy that Turkish soldiers would not be engaged in combat operations, and he said Turkey wished the United States well in its undertaking of Obama's new campaign strategy.

Meanwhile, Turkish President Abdullah Gul signaled that Turkey would expand its activities in Afghanistan but said that decision would be made by Ankara alone. "Sending soldiers is not the solution," Gul was quoted as saying. "We need to give equipment and training to Afghan forces. If Turkey sends combat forces to Afghanistan, the power that everybody respects — including [the] Taliban — will disappear." Gul apparently was suggesting that Turkey has considerable influence over the Pashtun jihadists — influence that the United States needs — and this would be undermined if Ankara joined the fighting in Afghanistan.

Gul went on to say that the international community is expecting Turkey to play a role in Afghanistan that no one else can play — namely, bringing the insurgents into the country's existing political framework. "We need to gain the heart of [the] Afghan people," he said. "This is not bird flu. How can you cope with it otherwise?" These statements suggest that the Turks not only are emphasizing their own diplomatic role in Afghanistan but also are arguing that the U.S. strategy to surge forces into the country will have a limited role in stabilizing the country.

There are other issues that limit Turkey's ability to send soldiers abroad — chief among them Kurdish separatism and the struggle with Greece over Cyprus. In short, the Turkish military's priority is the defense of its borders. There also is the matter of the government being constrained by widespread public sentiment in Turkey that is deeply opposed to U.S. invasions in the Muslim world.

This is not the first time Turkey has turned down a U.S. request to be involved in, or assist with, combat activity. In early 2003, in its first term, the Justice and Development (AK) Party government refused to allow the Bush administration to use Turkish soil for its invasion of Iraq after the Turkish Parliament overwhelmingly voted against the request. Given the limited Turkish military role in Afghanistan since late 2001, Ankara was not expected to drastically alter the nature of its involvement in the Afghan campaign.

Still, the Turkish decision is a disappointment for the Americans, considering how hard Obama has been pushing for enhanced relations, viewing Turkey as the power that can help the United States with a variety of issues around the globe, especially in the Middle East and the wider Islamic world. From the point of view of Ankara, however, it is utilizing its emerging status as a global player to avoid getting involved in risky areas that can upset its foreign policy calculus. After being in a geopolitical coma for almost a century, Turkey under the AK Party government is in the process of expanding its influence in virtually all the regions it straddles.

As it is, the Turks are having to engage in delicate balancing acts between the United States and Russia, the United States and Iran, and the Arab states and Israel, among other countries. And Turkey can afford to say no to the United States — a function of its intrinsic power and Washington's need for Ankara's help in many areas. Hence, Turkey is not interested in participating in any initiative that could upset its attempt to return to the world stage as a major player.

Turkey also recognizes the difficult U.S. situation in the Middle East and South Asia and wants to be able to keep itself at a safe distance so as not to become associated with what it views as American miscalculations. The Turkish military leadership is very concerned that U.S. policy in the region has failed and that Afghanistan is headed in the wrong direction. Being part of combat operations there would seriously undermine the position that Ankara is trying to create for itself in Afghanistan, Pakistan and Iran.

Not having a border with Afghanistan already places limits on Turkish influence in Afghanistan, as does the country's ethnic makeup. Turkic peoples (Uzbeks and Turkmens) represent only small minorities in Afghanistan — a handicap Turkey is trying to overcome by being an interlocutor between Kabul and the minorities (especially top Uzbek warlord Abdul Rashid Dostum), Kabul and Islamabad, and Kabul and Washington. The Turkish military contingent in Afghanistan — 1,750 troops — has been engaged in providing security and training Afghan National Police personnel in NATO's Regional Command in Kabul and the surrounding area.

Through these activities, Turkey is trying to establish a foothold in Afghanistan that it can later use to broaden its influence in Central Asia, whence the founders of the Ottoman Empire — predecessor to the modern Turkish republic — came in the early 14th century. But the Turks have long been gone from the region, which is far from Turkish borders and almost exclusively in Russia's sphere of influence. Turkey can go only so far in creating a space for itself in Central Asia. Afghanistan, however, could be a point of entry for the Turks to gain greater access to the region of its forefathers. The Turkmen, Uzbek and Tajik minorities in Afghanistan, along with the country's long borders with Turkmenistan, Uzbekistan and Tajikistan, could come in handy.

It will take a long time for Turkey to solidify its influence in these areas, and it cannot afford to get involved in the fight against the Taliban, which represent the most potent Afghan military force, or become entangled in conflict among the various Afghan ethnic groups. This is why Turkey will stick to its security and training role in Kabul, thereby fulfilling its NATO obligations and slowly broadening its geopolitical footprint in the region.

Moving Toward a Global Afghan Taliban Settlement
Jan. 26, 2010

Jan. 25, 2010, will be remembered as the day when much of the planet buzzed about diplomatic talks with Afghanistan's Taliban movement. The chatter comes in the context of a number of conferences that will be held over the course of the next week that focus on dealing with Afghanistan's jihadist insurgency. The countries being represented at the meetings — including the United States, the Central Asian states, Europe, Russia, Turkey, Saudi Arabia, Iran, Pakistan, India and China — have a stake in what happens in Afghanistan.

Each of these players has a different view on how to engage the Taliban in a negotiation process, but there seems to be an emerging consensus that when all is said and done, the Afghan jihadist movement — in one form or another — will be part of the government in Kabul. In other words, there is a general acceptance that if Afghanistan is to be settled, the Taliban have to be dealt with as legitimate political stakeholders. The difference lies in the degree to which the Taliban can be accepted.

From the point of view of the United States and its NATO allies, ideally the surge should be able to weaken the momentum of the Taliban and the overall counterinsurgency that divides them. This would result in a significant number of pragmatic elements being stripped from the core that surrounds Mullah Omar and other leaders. The United States and its Western allies are not, however, naive enough to believe that this can be achieved in the short span of time laid out in U.S. President Barack Obama's Afghanistan strategy. Therefore, the West could learn to live with the hard-line Taliban as long as they can separate themselves from al Qaeda, though there is still the matter of how the Obama administration will be able to sell this on the home front, especially in such a dicey political climate.

Pakistan, the second most important player when it comes to dealing with the Taliban (given Islamabad's historic ties to the

Afghan jihadists), would ideally like to see the Taliban gain a large share of the political pie in Kabul. Such an outcome could allow Islamabad to reverse the loss of its influence in Afghanistan and use a more Pakistan-friendly regime as a lever to deal with its security dilemma with India. That said, a political comeback of the Taliban in Afghanistan would also bring significant security threats to the Pakistani state, given Islamabad's own indigenous Taliban insurgency and the complexities that exist between the two.

Though it does not share a direct border with Afghanistan, India is the one country that seems completely opposed to accommodating the Taliban. New Delhi does not want to see the influence it has gained over the past eight years eroded. More important, it does not want Pakistan to get a breather in Afghanistan so that it can focus on the Kashmir issue. From India's point of view, an Afghan Taliban political revival could boost the regional anti-India Islamist militant landscape.

Iran, the other major power that shares a border with Afghanistan and has deep ethno-linguistic, sectarian, cultural and political ties with its eastern neighbor, has a complex strategy in relation to the Taliban. It is in Tehran's interest to back certain elements of the Afghan Taliban as doing so keeps the United States occupied — at least in the short term — with the war in Afghanistan. This keeps it from taking aggressive action against the Islamic republic over the nuclear issue. In the long run, though, the radical Persian Shia are ideological enemies of militant Pashtun Sunnis and would want to see them boxed in by any negotiated settlement. The Iranians will play a role in any such outcome, particularly through its proxies among the non-Pashtun minorities. Iran also does not want to see Saudi Arabia, its main regional rival, make gains in Afghanistan, given Riyadh's historical relations to the Taliban and Pakistan.

Conversely, for the Saudis there is no turning back the clock in Iraq, where an Iranian-leaning, Shia-dominated state has emerged. The Saudis are also seeing how Iran has made deep inroads to its north in Lebanon and south in Yemen and has potential proxies within the Shiite populations in the oil-rich Persian Gulf Arab states.

The rise of the Taliban, which has religious as well as ideological ties to the Saudis, could serve as a key means of countering Iranian moves against the oil-rich kingdom.

Turkmenistan, Uzbekistan and Tajikistan, the three Central Asian states that share borders with Afghanistan, have ties to their respective co-ethnic brethren in Afghanistan, and deep security concerns about a government with a Taliban presence. The Taliban, during their first stint in power, provided sanctuary to Islamist rebels from all across the steppes of Central Asia. Therefore, these three bordering states are relying on the U.S.-led international process to make sure that a resurgent Taliban can be kept in check.

They also have to contend with the reality that Russia, which enjoys a monopoly of influence in Central Asia, has an interest in the Taliban insurgency remaining a thorn in the side of the United States, at least long enough to make it difficult for Washington to extricate itself. As long as the United States remains bogged down in Afghanistan and other parts of the Islamic world, Russia has the freedom to effect its own geopolitical revival in the former Soviet Union. The Central Asian republics, however, do take comfort in the fact that in the long term, Russia sees the Taliban as a security threat to its Central Asian sphere of influence as well as the Caucasus.

China's position is similar to that of the Central Asian states. The Chinese fear that a legal Taliban presence in Afghanistan could help Uighur/East Turkestani Islamist militants with ties to Central Asian militants threaten the stability of their own Muslim northwest. But the Chinese have close ties to the Pakistanis and therefore will be working on both fronts to ensure that any Taliban political resurgence in Afghanistan is constrained.

Finally, there is Turkey, which has no physical links to the region but is using its influence with the United States, Afghanistan, Pakistan and, more recently, Iran to bring the various pieces of the Taliban juggernaut toward some settlement. Turkey under the Justice and Development Party is trying to insert itself as mediator in various conflicts within the Islamic world — a move endorsed by the United States, which needs all the help it can get. In this case, the Turkish government is using its deep ties to Afghanistan and Pakistan to connect the United States and NATO with the Taliban. This, coupled with Turkey's ethnic ties to Afghanistan's Uzbek and Turkmen communities, constitutes a means for Ankara to create a sphere of influence in the southwest Asian country, where it can serve as a potential jumping-off point to expand influence into Central Asia — the land of its forefathers and fellow Turkic peoples.

It is way too early to say what those with an interest in what becomes of the Afghan Taliban insurgency will do with this complex web of competing and conflicting geopolitical calculi as they move toward a settlement. They do not all have an equal say. The United States is the prime mover, and so all states must plan to align themselves with the United States' exit timetable. In a best-case scenario, some states will walk away with some gains and others will have to cut their losses. In a worst-case scenario, all of these efforts fail and Afghanistan descends into a state of nature where the balance of power is sorted out the old-fashioned way.

Russia, India: Coming Together Again Over Afghanistan
March 12, 2010

Russian Prime Minister Vladimir Putin visited New Delhi on March 11 to discuss, among other things, Afghanistan. During his visit, he is working with the Indians to formulate a common strategy for dealing with that country. Ahead of Putin's visit, Russian Ambassador to India Alexander Kadakin said it was time for NATO forces to withdraw from Afghanistan. He added that though Russia understands that may not happen immediately, both Russia and India are preparing to cooperate with one another to lay the groundwork for their policies in Afghanistan in anticipation of an eventual U.S. withdrawal.

With the United States turning its attention away from Iraq, Afghanistan is fast becoming — for the moment — a focal point of international attention. Washington is in the process of committing a total of nearly 100,000 troops to the campaign there for the next 12 to 18 months, and it remains the single most important focus of the NATO alliance. But while the U.S. focus has been in the process of shifting to Afghanistan for two years now, other countries such as India, Russia and Iran are beginning to focus their attention to the war-torn country for reasons of their own.

The nature of this focus is twofold. First there are international players like Iran that benefit from the fact that U.S. attention — particularly its ground combat capability — is being absorbed by Afghanistan. Keeping the U.S. bogged down there creates room for maneuver on other issues. Second, there are a number of countries that have an interest in the future of Afghanistan and will need to position themselves to take advantage of the duration of the expected U.S. commitment, a pivotal time for Afghanistan in terms of shaping the long-term realities of the country.

Enter the Russo-Indian alignment on Afghanistan. Much like Iran, Russia sees benefits in having the U.S. bogged down in Afghanistan. Russia's current drive to consolidate control over its periphery benefits greatly from the American distraction in the Middle East and South Asia. Logistical challenges for the United States in Afghanistan have created new levers for Moscow as Washington has sought supply routes through the former Soviet Union.

But Russia also must consider the long-term perspective on Afghanistan, a tumultuous country that borders its near abroad. To ensure that it does not face challenges in a post-withdrawal period, Russia will need to be prepared to deal with an American-Pakistani-Saudi-Turkish understanding and immense influence in the country.

As Russia seeks to counterbalance the United States in Afghanistan, India is seeking to counterbalance Pakistan. India has no border with Afghanistan, and it does not have many tools with which to challenge Pakistan's influence there head-on, so it — like Russia — has less influence in the country than it would prefer. A government in

Kabul friendly to Islamabad emboldens Pakistan by giving it a secure border, allowing it to focus all of its free attention to its east, whereas an Afghan government friendly to New Delhi weakens Pakistan.

Alliances between countries have a way of recurring throughout history because of the fundamental geopolitical and geographic factors that define a region. Russo-Indian cooperation on Afghanistan is no exception. New Delhi supported the Marxist governments of Kabul that existed during the 1980s at a time when a U.S.-Pakistani-Saudi alliance was supporting Islamist insurgents in bleeding the Red Army.

When the Taliban rose to power in the midst of the intra-Islamist civil war that erupted following the fall of the Marxist regime in 1992, both India and Russia, along with Iran, supported the anti-Taliban forces — largely made up of Tajiks, Hazara and Uzbeks — that formed the Northern Alliance. The three countries' common interest in opposing the rise of a Pashtun-dominated government in Kabul led them to support the same groups: The enemy of their common enemy became their common proxy. And just as Russia, Iran and India found themselves seeking a common strategy in the 1990s in the wake of Afghanistan's descent into civil war, so, too, will these countries seek to set themselves up as partners in their current attempts to influence the situation in Afghanistan.

Even together, Russia, Iran and India face a more powerful bloc with more influence than they could hope to achieve. But they are not without influence — not only among the ethnic minorities but also among the Pashtuns who were formerly affiliated with the Marxist regimes and through aid monies (India is the largest regional donor to Afghanistan). The U.S.-Pakistani-Saudi-Turkish alignment also is leaning heavily on Pakistan to use its immense influence to move forward with their plans for Afghanistan. Because this entails a deeper Islamist influence, both Russia and India will do what they can to cooperate and limit that accommodation, which could put them on a collision course with American efforts in Afghanistan.

At the heart of the issue is transnational Islamist militancy, which is the central thread of the common Russian, Iranian and Indian self-interest in Afghanistan. Pakistan has long cultivated militancy in the Pashtun regions on both sides of the Afghan-Pakistani border. Islamabad keeps these groups on hand as leverage against New Delhi — it was from these groups that the 2008 Mumbai attacks originated.

Similarly, Moscow's painful — and recent — memories of Chechen militancy have given rise to deep-seated fears about militancy along its periphery (not to mention that it was the Taliban regime in Afghanistan that was the only "government" to recognize Chechen "independence"). More important, the Russians are worried about the spillover of Islamist militancy from Afghanistan to Turkmenistan, Uzbekistan and Tajikistan — a more immediate threat given the shared borders. Now the U.S.-Pakistani-Saudi-Turkish axis is seeking, to one degree or another, to facilitate the political accommodation of Taliban and other Islamist groups into the regime in Kabul — the very groups over which Russia, Iran and India harbor the deepest concern.

—

Made in the USA
Lexington, KY
15 July 2010